50 Asian Fusion Taco Recipes for Home

By: Kelly Johnson

Table of Contents

- Korean BBQ Beef Bulgogi Tacos
- Vietnamese Lemongrass Chicken Tacos
- Japanese Miso-Glazed Pork Tacos
- Thai Red Curry Shrimp Tacos
- Chinese Five-Spice Duck Confit Tacos
- Indian Butter Chicken Tacos
- Filipino Adobo Pork Tacos
- Malaysian Satay Beef Tacos
- Indonesian Rendang Beef Tacos
- Thai Green Curry Tofu Tacos
- Korean Spicy Kimchi Pork Tacos
- Japanese Teriyaki Salmon Tacos
- Vietnamese Banh Mi Tacos with Grilled Pork
- Thai Basil Chicken Tacos
- Chinese Kung Pao Chicken Tacos
- Indian Tandoori Chicken Tacos
- Malaysian Sambal Shrimp Tacos
- Korean Bulgogi Tofu Tacos
- Japanese Tempura Shrimp Tacos
- Thai Peanut Chicken Tacos
- Chinese Orange Beef Tacos
- Vietnamese Pho Beef Tacos
- Indian Curry Lamb Tacos
- Malaysian Nasi Lemak Tacos
- Korean Dak Galbi Chicken Tacos
- Thai Coconut Curry Shrimp Tacos
- Japanese Tonkatsu Pork Tacos
- Filipino Adobo Chicken Tacos
- Chinese Sweet and Sour Tofu Tacos
- Indian Tikka Masala Tofu Tacos
- Malaysian Rendang Chicken Tacos
- Korean Japchae Beef Tacos
- Thai Mango Sticky Rice Tacos
- Japanese Okonomiyaki Tacos
- Vietnamese Caramelized Pork Belly Tacos

- Indian Vindaloo Beef Tacos
- Malaysian Laksa Shrimp Tacos
- Korean Dak Bulgogi Tacos
- Thai Pineapple Fried Rice Tacos
- Chinese General Tso's Chicken Tacos
- Filipino Sinigang Fish Tacos
- Indian Saag Paneer Tacos
- Malaysian Char Kway Teow Beef Tacos
- Korean Galbi Short Rib Tacos
- Thai Massaman Curry Beef Tacos
- Japanese Gyoza Tacos
- Vietnamese Bun Cha Pork Tacos
- Chinese Mapo Tofu Tacos
- Indian Chana Masala Tacos
- Malaysian Hainanese Chicken Rice Tacos

Korean BBQ Beef Bulgogi Tacos

Ingredients:

For the beef bulgogi:

- 1 lb beef sirloin or ribeye, thinly sliced
- 1/2 cup soy sauce
- 1/4 cup brown sugar
- 2 tablespoons sesame oil
- 3 cloves garlic, minced
- 1 tablespoon ginger, grated
- 2 green onions, chopped
- 1 tablespoon sesame seeds
- 1 tablespoon rice vinegar (optional)
- 1 tablespoon mirin (optional)
- 1 tablespoon gochujang (Korean chili paste) for added heat (optional)

For assembling tacos:

- 8-10 small flour or corn tortillas
- Shredded lettuce or cabbage
- Thinly sliced cucumber or radish
- Kimchi
- Sriracha or gochujang mayo (optional)
- Additional green onions and sesame seeds for garnish

Instructions:

1. Marinate the beef:
   - In a bowl, combine soy sauce, brown sugar, sesame oil, minced garlic, grated ginger, chopped green onions, sesame seeds, rice vinegar, mirin, and gochujang (if using). Mix well until the sugar is dissolved.
   - Add the thinly sliced beef to the marinade and toss until well coated. Cover and refrigerate for at least 1 hour, or preferably overnight, to allow the flavors to penetrate the meat.
2. Cook the beef bulgogi:

- Heat a skillet or grill over medium-high heat. Once hot, add the marinated beef slices in a single layer. Cook for 2-3 minutes on each side until caramelized and cooked through.
- Transfer the cooked beef bulgogi to a plate and let it rest for a few minutes before slicing it into bite-sized pieces.

3. Assemble the tacos:
   - Warm the tortillas in the skillet or grill for a few seconds on each side until soft and pliable.
   - Place a spoonful of shredded lettuce or cabbage on each tortilla, followed by a few slices of beef bulgogi.
   - Top with thinly sliced cucumber or radish, kimchi, and a drizzle of sriracha or gochujang mayo if desired.
   - Garnish with additional chopped green onions and sesame seeds.

4. Serve and enjoy:
   - Serve the Korean BBQ Beef Bulgogi Tacos immediately while warm, with extra kimchi and dipping sauce on the side if desired.
   - Enjoy the flavorful fusion of Korean and Mexican cuisines in every bite!

Vietnamese Lemongrass Chicken Tacos

Ingredients:

For the lemongrass chicken:

- 1 lb chicken breast or thigh, thinly sliced
- 2 stalks lemongrass, outer layers removed, finely chopped
- 3 cloves garlic, minced
- 1 shallot, minced
- 2 tablespoons soy sauce
- 1 tablespoon fish sauce
- 1 tablespoon brown sugar
- 1 tablespoon lime juice
- 1 tablespoon sesame oil
- 1 tablespoon vegetable oil
- Salt and pepper, to taste

For assembling tacos:

- 8-10 small flour or corn tortillas
- Shredded lettuce or cabbage
- Thinly sliced cucumber or pickled vegetables
- Fresh cilantro leaves
- Sriracha or chili garlic sauce (optional)
- Lime wedges, for serving

Instructions:

1. Marinate the chicken:
    - In a bowl, combine chopped lemongrass, minced garlic, minced shallot, soy sauce, fish sauce, brown sugar, lime juice, sesame oil, vegetable oil, salt, and pepper. Mix well to combine.
    - Add the thinly sliced chicken to the marinade and toss until evenly coated. Cover and refrigerate for at least 30 minutes, or up to 4 hours, to allow the flavors to meld.
2. Cook the lemongrass chicken:

- Heat a skillet or grill over medium-high heat. Once hot, add the marinated chicken slices in a single layer. Cook for 3-4 minutes on each side until cooked through and slightly charred.
- Transfer the cooked chicken to a plate and let it rest for a few minutes before slicing it into bite-sized pieces.

3. Assemble the tacos:
   - Warm the tortillas in the skillet or grill for a few seconds on each side until soft and pliable.
   - Place a spoonful of shredded lettuce or cabbage on each tortilla, followed by a few slices of lemongrass chicken.
   - Top with thinly sliced cucumber or pickled vegetables, fresh cilantro leaves, and a drizzle of sriracha or chili garlic sauce if desired.

4. Serve and enjoy:
   - Serve the Vietnamese Lemongrass Chicken Tacos immediately while warm, with lime wedges on the side for squeezing over the tacos.
   - Enjoy the burst of flavors and textures in every bite of these delicious fusion tacos!

Japanese Miso-Glazed Pork Tacos

Ingredients:

For the miso-glazed pork:

- 1 lb pork tenderloin, thinly sliced
- 3 tablespoons white miso paste
- 2 tablespoons soy sauce
- 2 tablespoons mirin (Japanese sweet rice wine)
- 2 tablespoons sake (Japanese rice wine) or dry white wine
- 2 tablespoons brown sugar
- 1 tablespoon sesame oil
- 2 cloves garlic, minced
- 1 teaspoon grated fresh ginger
- 1 tablespoon vegetable oil

For assembling tacos:

- 8-10 small flour or corn tortillas
- Shredded cabbage or lettuce
- Sliced avocado
- Thinly sliced radishes
- Chopped green onions
- Sesame seeds, for garnish
- Sriracha mayo or Japanese mayo (optional)
- Lime wedges, for serving

Instructions:

1. Prepare the miso glaze:
    - In a bowl, combine white miso paste, soy sauce, mirin, sake, brown sugar, sesame oil, minced garlic, and grated ginger. Mix well until smooth and well combined.
2. Marinate the pork:
    - Place the thinly sliced pork tenderloin in a shallow dish or resealable plastic bag. Pour the miso glaze over the pork, ensuring that each slice is

coated evenly. Cover or seal and refrigerate for at least 30 minutes, or up to 4 hours, to allow the flavors to meld.
3. Cook the pork:
    - Heat vegetable oil in a skillet or grill pan over medium-high heat. Once hot, add the marinated pork slices in a single layer. Cook for 2-3 minutes on each side until caramelized and cooked through.
4. Assemble the tacos:
    - Warm the tortillas in the skillet or grill for a few seconds on each side until soft and pliable.
    - Place a spoonful of shredded cabbage or lettuce on each tortilla, followed by a few slices of miso-glazed pork.
    - Top with sliced avocado, thinly sliced radishes, chopped green onions, and a sprinkle of sesame seeds.
    - Drizzle with sriracha mayo or Japanese mayo if desired.
5. Serve and enjoy:
    - Serve the Japanese Miso-Glazed Pork Tacos immediately while warm, with lime wedges on the side for squeezing over the tacos.
    - Enjoy the unique fusion of Japanese and Mexican flavors in every bite!

Thai Red Curry Shrimp Tacos

Ingredients:

For the red curry shrimp:

- 1 lb large shrimp, peeled and deveined
- 2 tablespoons Thai red curry paste
- 1 can (13.5 oz) coconut milk
- 2 tablespoons fish sauce
- 1 tablespoon brown sugar
- 1 tablespoon lime juice
- 2 cloves garlic, minced
- 1 tablespoon vegetable oil

For assembling tacos:

- 8-10 small flour or corn tortillas
- Shredded cabbage or lettuce
- Sliced cucumber
- Sliced red bell pepper
- Fresh cilantro leaves
- Lime wedges, for serving

Instructions:

1. Prepare the red curry shrimp:
    - In a bowl, mix together Thai red curry paste, coconut milk, fish sauce, brown sugar, and lime juice until well combined.
    - Heat vegetable oil in a skillet over medium heat. Add minced garlic and cook for 1 minute until fragrant.
    - Add the shrimp to the skillet and cook for 2-3 minutes until they start to turn pink.
    - Pour the red curry mixture over the shrimp and simmer for another 2-3 minutes until the shrimp are cooked through and the sauce has thickened slightly. Remove from heat.
2. Assemble the tacos:
    - Warm the tortillas in a skillet or microwave until soft and pliable.
    - Place a spoonful of shredded cabbage or lettuce on each tortilla.
    - Add a few spoonfuls of the red curry shrimp mixture onto the cabbage.
    - Top with sliced cucumber, sliced red bell pepper, and fresh cilantro leaves.

3. Serve and enjoy:
    - Serve the Thai Red Curry Shrimp Tacos immediately, with lime wedges on the side for squeezing over the tacos.
    - Enjoy the explosion of flavors in every bite of these delicious Thai-inspired tacos!

Chinese Five-Spice Duck Confit Tacos

Ingredients:

For the duck confit:

- 2 duck legs (about 1 lb total)
- 2 tablespoons Chinese five-spice powder
- 2 cloves garlic, minced
- 2 tablespoons coarse salt
- 1 tablespoon sugar
- Zest of 1 orange
- Vegetable oil, for cooking

For assembling tacos:

- 8-10 small flour or corn tortillas
- Hoisin sauce
- Sliced cucumber
- Sliced scallions
- Chopped cilantro
- Sesame seeds, for garnish
- Lime wedges, for serving

Instructions:

1. Prepare the duck confit:
    - In a bowl, mix together Chinese five-spice powder, minced garlic, coarse salt, sugar, and orange zest.
    - Rub the spice mixture all over the duck legs, ensuring they are well coated. Cover and refrigerate for at least 12 hours, or up to 24 hours, to allow the flavors to penetrate the meat.
    - Preheat the oven to 300°F (150°C).
    - Rinse the duck legs under cold water to remove excess salt and spices. Pat dry with paper towels.
    - Heat a tablespoon of vegetable oil in an oven-safe skillet over medium-high heat. Add the duck legs, skin-side down, and cook for 3-4 minutes until the skin is golden brown and crispy.

- Flip the duck legs over and transfer the skillet to the preheated oven. Roast for 2-2.5 hours until the meat is tender and falls off the bone.
2. Shred the duck meat:
    - Remove the duck legs from the oven and let them cool slightly. Once cool enough to handle, shred the meat using two forks, discarding the bones and excess fat.
3. Assemble the tacos:
    - Warm the tortillas in a skillet or microwave until soft and pliable.
    - Spread a thin layer of hoisin sauce on each tortilla.
    - Add a generous portion of shredded duck meat onto each tortilla.
    - Top with sliced cucumber, sliced scallions, and chopped cilantro.
    - Sprinkle with sesame seeds for garnish.
4. Serve and enjoy:
    - Serve the Chinese Five-Spice Duck Confit Tacos immediately, with lime wedges on the side for squeezing over the tacos.
    - Enjoy the unique fusion of Chinese and Mexican flavors in every delicious bite!

Indian Butter Chicken Tacos

Ingredients:

For the butter chicken:

- 1 lb boneless, skinless chicken thighs or breasts, cut into bite-sized pieces
- 1 cup plain yogurt
- 2 tablespoons lemon juice
- 2 tablespoons garam masala
- 1 tablespoon ground turmeric
- 1 tablespoon ground cumin
- 1 tablespoon paprika
- 1 tablespoon ground coriander
- 2 teaspoons ground cinnamon
- 2 teaspoons ground black pepper
- 1 teaspoon ground ginger
- 1 teaspoon cayenne pepper (adjust to taste)
- 4 tablespoons unsalted butter
- 1 onion, finely chopped
- 4 cloves garlic, minced
- 1 tablespoon grated fresh ginger
- 1 can (14 oz) diced tomatoes
- 1 cup heavy cream
- Salt, to taste
- Fresh cilantro, chopped, for garnish

For assembling tacos:

- 8-10 small flour or corn tortillas
- Shredded lettuce or cabbage
- Sliced cucumber
- Sliced red onion
- Mango salsa or diced mango (optional)
- Lime wedges, for serving

Instructions:

1. Marinate the chicken:

- In a bowl, combine plain yogurt, lemon juice, garam masala, turmeric, cumin, paprika, coriander, cinnamon, black pepper, ground ginger, and cayenne pepper. Mix well.
- Add the chicken pieces to the marinade, ensuring they are well coated. Cover and refrigerate for at least 1 hour, or overnight for best results.

2. Cook the butter chicken:
    - In a large skillet or saucepan, melt the butter over medium heat. Add the finely chopped onion and cook until softened and translucent.
    - Add the minced garlic and grated ginger to the skillet and cook for another minute until fragrant.
    - Add the marinated chicken pieces to the skillet, along with any remaining marinade. Cook until the chicken is browned on all sides.
    - Stir in the diced tomatoes (with their juices) and heavy cream. Bring the mixture to a simmer and let it cook for 10-15 minutes, stirring occasionally, until the chicken is cooked through and the sauce has thickened.
    - Season with salt to taste. Remove from heat and garnish with chopped fresh cilantro.

3. Assemble the tacos:
    - Warm the tortillas in a skillet or microwave until soft and pliable.
    - Place a spoonful of shredded lettuce or cabbage on each tortilla.
    - Add a generous portion of butter chicken onto the lettuce.
    - Top with sliced cucumber, sliced red onion, and mango salsa or diced mango if using.

4. Serve and enjoy:
    - Serve the Indian Butter Chicken Tacos immediately, with lime wedges on the side for squeezing over the tacos.
    - Enjoy the delicious fusion of Indian and Mexican flavors in every bite!

Filipino Adobo Pork Tacos

Ingredients:

For the adobo pork:

- 1 lb pork shoulder, cut into bite-sized pieces
- 1/2 cup soy sauce
- 1/2 cup white vinegar
- 1/4 cup water
- 4 cloves garlic, minced
- 2 bay leaves
- 1 teaspoon whole peppercorns
- 1 tablespoon brown sugar
- 1 tablespoon vegetable oil

For assembling tacos:

- 8-10 small flour or corn tortillas
- Shredded lettuce or cabbage
- Sliced avocado
- Pickled red onions
- Chopped cilantro
- Lime wedges, for serving

Instructions:

1. Prepare the adobo pork:
    - In a large bowl, combine soy sauce, white vinegar, water, minced garlic, bay leaves, whole peppercorns, and brown sugar. Mix well to combine.
    - Add the pork shoulder pieces to the marinade, ensuring they are well coated. Cover and refrigerate for at least 1 hour, or overnight for best results.
2. Cook the adobo pork:
    - Heat vegetable oil in a large skillet or Dutch oven over medium-high heat. Once hot, add the marinated pork along with the marinade.

- Bring the mixture to a boil, then reduce the heat to low and let it simmer, covered, for about 45 minutes to 1 hour, stirring occasionally, until the pork is tender and the sauce has thickened.
3. Assemble the tacos:
    - Warm the tortillas in a skillet or microwave until soft and pliable.
    - Place a spoonful of shredded lettuce or cabbage on each tortilla.
    - Add a generous portion of adobo pork onto the lettuce.
    - Top with sliced avocado, pickled red onions, and chopped cilantro.
4. Serve and enjoy:
    - Serve the Filipino Adobo Pork Tacos immediately, with lime wedges on the side for squeezing over the tacos.
    - Enjoy the delicious fusion of Filipino and Mexican flavors in every bite!

Malaysian Satay Beef Tacos

Ingredients:

For the satay beef:

- 1 lb beef sirloin or flank steak, thinly sliced
- 1/4 cup soy sauce
- 2 tablespoons brown sugar
- 2 tablespoons lime juice
- 2 cloves garlic, minced
- 1 teaspoon ground turmeric
- 1 teaspoon ground coriander
- 1 teaspoon ground cumin
- 1/2 teaspoon ground ginger
- 1/2 teaspoon chili powder
- 1/4 teaspoon ground cinnamon
- 1/4 teaspoon ground nutmeg
- Wooden skewers, soaked in water for 30 minutes

For assembling tacos:

- 8-10 small flour or corn tortillas
- Shredded lettuce or cabbage
- Sliced cucumber
- Thinly sliced red onion
- Chopped peanuts, for garnish
- Chopped cilantro, for garnish
- Lime wedges, for serving

Instructions:

1. Marinate the beef:
    - In a bowl, combine soy sauce, brown sugar, lime juice, minced garlic, ground turmeric, ground coriander, ground cumin, ground ginger, chili powder, ground cinnamon, and ground nutmeg. Mix well.
    - Add the thinly sliced beef to the marinade, ensuring it is well coated. Cover and refrigerate for at least 1 hour, or overnight for best results.
2. Prepare the satay beef:
    - Preheat the grill or grill pan to medium-high heat.

- Thread the marinated beef slices onto the soaked wooden skewers, dividing evenly.
- Grill the skewers for 2-3 minutes on each side until the beef is cooked to your desired doneness and has grill marks.

3. Assemble the tacos:
   - Warm the tortillas in a skillet or microwave until soft and pliable.
   - Place a spoonful of shredded lettuce or cabbage on each tortilla.
   - Slide the grilled satay beef off the skewers and onto the tortillas.
   - Top with sliced cucumber, thinly sliced red onion, chopped peanuts, and chopped cilantro.
4. Serve and enjoy:
   - Serve the Malaysian Satay Beef Tacos immediately, with lime wedges on the side for squeezing over the tacos.
   - Enjoy the fusion of Malaysian and Mexican flavors in every bite!

Indonesian Rendang Beef Tacos

Ingredients:

For the rendang beef:

- 1 lb beef chuck or brisket, cut into bite-sized pieces
- 2 tablespoons vegetable oil
- 1 onion, finely chopped
- 4 cloves garlic, minced
- 1-inch piece of ginger, grated
- 2 lemongrass stalks, bruised and chopped into 2-inch pieces
- 4 kaffir lime leaves
- 1 cinnamon stick
- 4 cardamom pods, lightly crushed
- 4 cloves
- 1 teaspoon ground turmeric
- 1 tablespoon ground coriander
- 1 teaspoon ground cumin
- 1 teaspoon chili powder
- 1 tablespoon tamarind paste
- 1 can (14 oz) coconut milk
- Salt, to taste
- Brown sugar, to taste
- Lime wedges, for serving
- Chopped cilantro, for garnish

For assembling tacos:

- 8-10 small flour or corn tortillas
- Sliced cucumber
- Sliced red onion
- Sliced jalapenos (optional)
- Fresh cilantro leaves
- Lime wedges, for serving

Instructions:

1. Prepare the rendang beef:

- Heat the vegetable oil in a large skillet or Dutch oven over medium heat. Add the chopped onion, minced garlic, and grated ginger. Cook until softened and fragrant.
- Add the lemongrass, kaffir lime leaves, cinnamon stick, cardamom pods, cloves, ground turmeric, ground coriander, ground cumin, and chili powder to the skillet. Cook, stirring frequently, for 2-3 minutes until the spices are fragrant.
- Add the beef pieces to the skillet and cook until browned on all sides.
- Stir in the tamarind paste and coconut milk. Bring the mixture to a simmer.
- Reduce the heat to low and let the beef simmer, uncovered, for 2-3 hours until the beef is tender and the sauce has thickened. Stir occasionally to prevent sticking.
- Season with salt and brown sugar to taste. Remove the lemongrass stalks, kaffir lime leaves, cinnamon stick, and cardamom pods before serving.

2. Assemble the tacos:
   - Warm the tortillas in a skillet or microwave until soft and pliable.
   - Place a spoonful of rendang beef onto each tortilla.
   - Top with sliced cucumber, sliced red onion, sliced jalapenos (if using), and fresh cilantro leaves.

3. Serve and enjoy:
   - Serve the Indonesian Rendang Beef Tacos immediately, with lime wedges on the side for squeezing over the tacos.
   - Enjoy the delicious fusion of Indonesian and Mexican flavors in every bite!

Thai Green Curry Tofu Tacos

Ingredients:

For the Thai green curry tofu:

- 1 block (14 oz) extra-firm tofu, pressed and cubed
- 2 tablespoons Thai green curry paste
- 1 can (14 oz) coconut milk
- 1 tablespoon soy sauce
- 1 tablespoon brown sugar
- 1 tablespoon lime juice
- 1 bell pepper, thinly sliced
- 1 small zucchini, thinly sliced
- 1 cup sliced mushrooms
- 1 tablespoon vegetable oil
- Salt, to taste
- Fresh cilantro leaves, for garnish

For assembling tacos:

- 8-10 small flour or corn tortillas
- Shredded lettuce or cabbage
- Sliced avocado
- Thinly sliced red onion
- Chopped peanuts, for garnish
- Lime wedges, for serving

Instructions:

1. Prepare the Thai green curry tofu:
   - In a large skillet or wok, heat vegetable oil over medium-high heat. Add cubed tofu and cook until golden brown and crispy on all sides. Remove from the skillet and set aside.
   - In the same skillet, add Thai green curry paste and cook for 1-2 minutes until fragrant.
   - Stir in coconut milk, soy sauce, brown sugar, and lime juice. Bring to a simmer.

- Add sliced bell pepper, zucchini, and mushrooms to the skillet. Cook for 3-4 minutes until vegetables are tender-crisp.
- Return the cooked tofu to the skillet and stir to coat it with the green curry sauce. Cook for another 2-3 minutes until heated through. Season with salt to taste.

2. Assemble the tacos:
   - Warm the tortillas in a skillet or microwave until soft and pliable.
   - Place a spoonful of shredded lettuce or cabbage on each tortilla.
   - Add a generous portion of Thai green curry tofu and vegetables onto the lettuce.
   - Top with sliced avocado, thinly sliced red onion, and chopped peanuts.
3. Serve and enjoy:
   - Serve the Thai Green Curry Tofu Tacos immediately, with lime wedges on the side for squeezing over the tacos.
   - Garnish with fresh cilantro leaves for added flavor and color.
   - Enjoy the delicious fusion of Thai and Mexican flavors in every bite!

Korean Spicy Kimchi Pork Tacos

Ingredients:

For the spicy kimchi pork:

- 1 lb pork belly or pork shoulder, thinly sliced
- 1 cup kimchi, chopped
- 2 tablespoons gochujang (Korean chili paste)
- 2 tablespoons soy sauce
- 1 tablespoon sesame oil
- 2 cloves garlic, minced
- 1 tablespoon brown sugar
- 1 tablespoon rice vinegar
- 1 tablespoon vegetable oil
- 1 green onion, thinly sliced (for garnish)

For assembling tacos:

- 8-10 small flour or corn tortillas
- Shredded lettuce or cabbage
- Sliced cucumber
- Thinly sliced radishes
- Sesame seeds, for garnish
- Lime wedges, for serving

Instructions:

1. Prepare the spicy kimchi pork:
    - In a bowl, combine chopped kimchi, gochujang, soy sauce, sesame oil, minced garlic, brown sugar, and rice vinegar. Mix well.
    - Add the thinly sliced pork to the marinade, ensuring it is well coated. Cover and refrigerate for at least 30 minutes, or up to 2 hours, to allow the flavors to meld.
    - Heat vegetable oil in a large skillet or wok over medium-high heat. Add the marinated pork and cook for 5-7 minutes until cooked through and slightly caramelized.
2. Assemble the tacos:
    - Warm the tortillas in a skillet or microwave until soft and pliable.
    - Place a spoonful of shredded lettuce or cabbage on each tortilla.
    - Add a generous portion of spicy kimchi pork onto the lettuce.
    - Top with sliced cucumber, thinly sliced radishes, and a sprinkle of sesame seeds.

    - Garnish with thinly sliced green onions.
3. Serve and enjoy:
    - Serve the Korean Spicy Kimchi Pork Tacos immediately, with lime wedges on the side for squeezing over the tacos.
    - Enjoy the delicious fusion of Korean and Mexican flavors in every bite!

Japanese Teriyaki Salmon Tacos

Ingredients:

For the teriyaki salmon:

- 1 lb salmon fillets, skin removed
- 1/4 cup soy sauce
- 2 tablespoons mirin
- 2 tablespoons sake (or dry white wine)
- 2 tablespoons brown sugar
- 2 cloves garlic, minced
- 1 teaspoon grated ginger
- 1 tablespoon vegetable oil

For assembling tacos:

- 8-10 small flour or corn tortillas
- Shredded cabbage or lettuce
- Sliced avocado
- Thinly sliced cucumber
- Sesame seeds, for garnish
- Thinly sliced green onions, for garnish
- Lime wedges, for serving

Instructions:

1. Prepare the teriyaki salmon:
    - In a small bowl, whisk together soy sauce, mirin, sake, brown sugar, minced garlic, and grated ginger to make the teriyaki sauce.
    - Place the salmon fillets in a shallow dish and pour half of the teriyaki sauce over them. Reserve the remaining sauce for later.
    - Marinate the salmon fillets in the refrigerator for at least 30 minutes, or up to 1 hour.
2. Cook the salmon:
    - Heat vegetable oil in a large skillet over medium-high heat. Remove the salmon fillets from the marinade and shake off any excess.

- Place the salmon fillets in the skillet, skin-side down, and cook for 3-4 minutes until the skin is crispy and golden brown.
- Flip the salmon fillets over and cook for an additional 2-3 minutes until cooked through. Remove from heat.

3. Assemble the tacos:
   - Warm the tortillas in a skillet or microwave until soft and pliable.
   - Place a spoonful of shredded cabbage or lettuce on each tortilla.
   - Flake the cooked teriyaki salmon and divide it evenly among the tortillas.
   - Top each taco with sliced avocado and thinly sliced cucumber.
   - Drizzle the reserved teriyaki sauce over the tacos.
   - Garnish with sesame seeds and thinly sliced green onions.

4. Serve and enjoy:
   - Serve the Japanese Teriyaki Salmon Tacos immediately, with lime wedges on the side for squeezing over the tacos.
   - Enjoy the delicious fusion of Japanese and Mexican flavors in every bite!

Vietnamese Banh Mi Tacos with Grilled Pork

Ingredients:

For the grilled pork:

- 1 lb pork shoulder or pork tenderloin, thinly sliced
- 3 tablespoons soy sauce
- 2 tablespoons fish sauce
- 2 tablespoons brown sugar
- 2 cloves garlic, minced
- 1 shallot, minced
- 1 tablespoon vegetable oil

For assembling tacos:

- 8-10 small flour or corn tortillas
- Pickled carrots and daikon (or thinly sliced radishes)
- Sliced cucumber
- Sliced jalapenos
- Fresh cilantro leaves
- Sliced green onions
- Sriracha mayo or aioli
- Lime wedges, for serving

Instructions:

1. Marinate and grill the pork:
    - In a bowl, combine soy sauce, fish sauce, brown sugar, minced garlic, and minced shallot. Mix well to make the marinade.
    - Add the thinly sliced pork to the marinade, ensuring it is well coated. Cover and refrigerate for at least 30 minutes, or up to 2 hours.
    - Heat vegetable oil in a grill pan or skillet over medium-high heat. Remove the pork from the marinade and grill for 2-3 minutes on each side until cooked through and slightly charred. Remove from heat and set aside.
2. Assemble the tacos:
    - Warm the tortillas in a skillet or microwave until soft and pliable.
    - Place a spoonful of pickled carrots and daikon on each tortilla.
    - Add a few slices of grilled pork onto the pickled vegetables.

    - Top with sliced cucumber, sliced jalapenos, fresh cilantro leaves, and s iced green onions.
    - Drizzle with sriracha mayo or aioli for added flavor.
3. Serve and enjoy:
    - Serve the Vietnamese Banh Mi Tacos with Grilled Pork immediately, with lime wedges on the side for squeezing over the tacos.
    - Enjoy the delicious fusion of Vietnamese and Mexican flavors in every bite!

Thai Basil Chicken Tacos

Ingredients:

For the Thai basil chicken:

- 1 lb boneless, skinless chicken breasts or thighs, thinly sliced
- 2 tablespoons vegetable oil
- 3 cloves garlic, minced
- 1 red chili pepper, thinly sliced
- 1 bell pepper, thinly sliced
- 1 onion, thinly sliced
- 1 cup fresh Thai basil leaves
- 2 tablespoons soy sauce
- 1 tablespoon fish sauce
- 1 tablespoon oyster sauce
- 1 tablespoon brown sugar
- 1 tablespoon lime juice
- Salt and pepper, to taste

For assembling tacos:

- 8-10 small flour or corn tortillas
- Shredded lettuce or cabbage
- Sliced cucumber
- Sliced red onion
- Fresh cilantro leaves
- Lime wedges, for serving

Instructions:

1. Prepare the Thai basil chicken:
    - Heat vegetable oil in a large skillet or wok over medium-high heat.
    - Add minced garlic and sliced red chili pepper to the skillet. Cook for 1-2 minutes until fragrant.
    - Add thinly sliced chicken to the skillet and cook until browned and cooked through.

- Stir in thinly sliced bell pepper and onion. Cook for another 2-3 minutes until vegetables are tender-crisp.
  - Add soy sauce, fish sauce, oyster sauce, brown sugar, and lime juice to the skillet. Stir to combine and cook for 1-2 minutes.
  - Remove from heat and stir in fresh Thai basil leaves. Season with salt and pepper to taste.
2. Assemble the tacos:
   - Warm the tortillas in a skillet or microwave until soft and pliable.
   - Place a spoonful of shredded lettuce or cabbage on each tortilla.
   - Add a generous portion of Thai basil chicken onto the lettuce.
   - Top with sliced cucumber, sliced red onion, and fresh cilantro leaves.
3. Serve and enjoy:
   - Serve the Thai Basil Chicken Tacos immediately, with lime wedges on the side for squeezing over the tacos.
   - Enjoy the delicious fusion of Thai and Mexican flavors in every bite!

Chinese Kung Pao Chicken Tacos

Ingredients:

For the Kung Pao Chicken:

- 1 lb boneless, skinless chicken breasts or thighs, cut into bite-sized pieces
- 2 tablespoons vegetable oil
- 3 cloves garlic, minced
- 1-inch piece of ginger, minced
- 1/2 cup unsalted peanuts
- 2-3 dried red chili peppers
- 1 bell pepper, diced
- 1/2 cup diced onion
- 2 green onions, chopped (white and green parts separated)
- 1/4 cup soy sauce
- 2 tablespoons rice vinegar
- 1 tablespoon hoisin sauce
- 1 tablespoon oyster sauce
- 1 tablespoon brown sugar
- 1 teaspoon cornstarch mixed with 1 tablespoon water (optional, for thickening)

For assembling tacos:

- 8-10 small flour or corn tortillas
- Shredded lettuce or cabbage
- Sliced cucumber
- Sliced red onion
- Fresh cilantro leaves
- Lime wedges, for serving

Instructions:

1. Prepare the Kung Pao Chicken:
    - Heat vegetable oil in a large skillet or wok over medium-high heat.
    - Add minced garlic and ginger to the skillet. Cook for 1-2 minutes until fragrant.
    - Add chicken pieces to the skillet and cook until browned and cooked through.
    - Stir in unsalted peanuts and dried red chili peppers. Cook for another 1-2 minutes.
    - Add diced bell pepper, diced onion, and the white parts of the chopped green onions to the skillet. Cook for 2-3 minutes until vegetables are tender-crisp.

- In a small bowl, mix together soy sauce, rice vinegar, hoisin sauce, oyster sauce, and brown sugar. Pour the sauce over the chicken and vegetables. Stir to combine.
- If desired, add the cornstarch-water mixture to the skillet to thicken the sauce. Cook for an additional 1-2 minutes until the sauce has thickened slightly.
- Remove from heat and garnish with the green parts of the chopped green onions.

2. Assemble the tacos:
   - Warm the tortillas in a skillet or microwave until soft and pliable.
   - Place a spoonful of shredded lettuce or cabbage on each tortilla.
   - Add a generous portion of Kung Pao Chicken onto the lettuce.
   - Top with sliced cucumber, sliced red onion, and fresh cilantro leaves.

3. Serve and enjoy:
   - Serve the Chinese Kung Pao Chicken Tacos immediately, with lime wedges on the side for squeezing over the tacos.
   - Enjoy the delicious fusion of Chinese and Mexican flavors in every bite!

Indian Tandoori Chicken Tacos

Ingredients:

For the Tandoori Chicken:

- 1 lb chicken breast, cut into thin strips
- 1 cup plain yogurt
- 2 tablespoons lemon juice
- 2 tablespoons Tandoori masala spice mix
- 1 tablespoon minced garlic
- 1 tablespoon minced ginger
- 1 teaspoon ground cumin
- 1 teaspoon ground coriander
- 1 teaspoon paprika
- Salt, to taste
- Vegetable oil, for cooking

For assembling tacos:

- 8-10 small flour or corn tortillas
- Shredded lettuce or cabbage
- Sliced cucumber
- Sliced red onion
- Chopped cilantro
- Lime wedges, for serving

Instructions:

1. Marinate the Tandoori Chicken:
    - In a bowl, combine yogurt, lemon juice, Tandoori masala spice mix, minced garlic, minced ginger, ground cumin, ground coriander, paprika, and salt.
    - Add the chicken strips to the marinade, ensuring they are well coated. Cover and refrigerate for at least 2 hours, or overnight for best results.
2. Cook the Tandoori Chicken:
    - Preheat the grill or grill pan over medium-high heat.
    - Thread the marinated chicken strips onto skewers or simply grill them directly.
    - Grill the chicken for 5-7 minutes on each side, or until cooked through and slightly charred. Remove from the grill and let it rest for a few minutes.
3. Assemble the tacos:

- Warm the tortillas in a skillet or microwave until soft and pliable.
- Place a spoonful of shredded lettuce or cabbage on each tortilla.
- Add a few pieces of Tandoori chicken onto the lettuce.
- Top with sliced cucumber, sliced red onion, and chopped cilantro.

4. Serve and enjoy:
    - Serve the Indian Tandoori Chicken Tacos immediately, with lime wedges on the side for squeezing over the tacos.
    - Enjoy the fusion of Indian and Mexican flavors in every bite! Adjust the toppings according to your preference, such as adding yogurt sauce or mango salsa for extra flavor.

Malaysian Sambal Shrimp Tacos

Ingredients:

For the Sambal Shrimp:

- 1 lb large shrimp, peeled and deveined
- 2 tablespoons vegetable oil
- 3 tablespoons sambal oelek (Malaysian chili paste)
- 2 cloves garlic, minced
- 1 tablespoon brown sugar
- 1 tablespoon soy sauce
- 1 tablespoon lime juice
- Salt, to taste
- Chopped cilantro, for garnish

For assembling tacos:

- 8-10 small flour or corn tortillas
- Shredded cabbage or lettuce
- Sliced cucumber
- Sliced red onion
- Lime wedges, for serving

Instructions:

1. Prepare the Sambal Shrimp:
    - Heat vegetable oil in a large skillet over medium-high heat.
    - Add minced garlic and sambal oelek to the skillet. Cook for 1-2 minutes until fragrant.
    - Add shrimp to the skillet and cook for 2-3 minutes until they start to turn pink.
    - Stir in brown sugar, soy sauce, and lime juice. Cook for another 1-2 minutes until the shrimp are cooked through and coated in the sauce.
    - Season with salt to taste. Remove from heat and set aside.
2. Assemble the tacos:
    - Warm the tortillas in a skillet or microwave until soft and pliable.
    - Place a spoonful of shredded cabbage or lettuce on each tortilla.
    - Add a few sambal shrimp onto the cabbage.
    - Top with sliced cucumber and sliced red onion.
3. Serve and enjoy:

- Serve the Malaysian Sambal Shrimp Tacos immediately, with lime wedges on the side for squeezing over the tacos.
- Garnish with chopped cilantro for added freshness and flavor.
- Enjoy the delicious fusion of Malaysian and Mexican flavors in every bite! Adjust the spiciness of the sambal according to your preference.

Korean Bulgogi Tofu Tacos

Ingredients:

For the Bulgogi Tofu:

- 1 block extra-firm tofu, pressed and sliced into thin strips
- 2 tablespoons soy sauce
- 1 tablespoon sesame oil
- 1 tablespoon brown sugar
- 1 tablespoon rice vinegar
- 2 cloves garlic, minced
- 1 teaspoon grated ginger
- 2 green onions, thinly sliced
- 1 tablespoon vegetable oil, for cooking

For assembling tacos:

- 8-10 small flour or corn tortillas
- Shredded lettuce or cabbage
- Sliced cucumber
- Julienned carrots
- Thinly sliced red onion
- Toasted sesame seeds, for garnish
- Sriracha mayo or Korean hot pepper paste (gochujang), for topping
- Lime wedges, for serving

Instructions:

1. Prepare the Bulgogi Tofu:
    - In a bowl, whisk together soy sauce, sesame oil, brown sugar, rice vinegar, minced garlic, grated ginger, and sliced green onions to make the marinade.
    - Add the sliced tofu to the marinade, ensuring it is well coated. Let it marinate for at least 30 minutes, or longer for more flavor.
    - Heat vegetable oil in a large skillet over medium-high heat. Add the marinated tofu and cook for 5-7 minutes, stirring occasionally, until browned and slightly caramelized. Remove from heat and set aside.
2. Assemble the Tacos:
    - Warm the tortillas in a skillet or microwave until soft and pliable.
    - Place a spoonful of shredded lettuce or cabbage on each tortilla.

- Add a few pieces of bulgogi tofu onto the lettuce.
- Top with sliced cucumber, julienned carrots, and thinly sliced red onion.
- Drizzle with sriracha mayo or Korean hot pepper paste (gochujang) for an extra kick.
- Garnish with toasted sesame seeds for added flavor and texture.

3. Serve and Enjoy:
    - Serve the Korean Bulgogi Tofu Tacos immediately, with lime wedges on the side for squeezing over the tacos.
    - Enjoy the delicious fusion of Korean and Mexican flavors in every bite! Adjust the toppings and spiciness according to your preference.

Japanese Tempura Shrimp Tacos

Ingredients:

For the Tempura Shrimp:

- 1 lb large shrimp, peeled and deveined
- 1 cup all-purpose flour
- 1/2 cup cornstarch
- 1 teaspoon baking powder
- 1 cup ice-cold water
- Vegetable oil, for frying

For assembling tacos:

- 8-10 small flour or corn tortillas
- Shredded cabbage or lettuce
- Sliced avocado
- Sliced cucumber
- Thinly sliced radishes
- Sriracha mayo or spicy mayo, for topping
- Soy sauce or ponzu sauce, for drizzling
- Lime wedges, for serving

Instructions:

1. Prepare the Tempura Shrimp:
    - In a large bowl, whisk together all-purpose flour, cornstarch, and baking powder.
    - Gradually add ice-cold water to the flour mixture, stirring until smooth. The batter should be thin and pourable but still slightly lumpy.
    - Heat vegetable oil in a deep fryer or large pot to 350°F (180°C).
    - Dip the shrimp into the tempura batter, coating them evenly.
    - Carefully place the battered shrimp into the hot oil, frying in batches to avoid overcrowding. Fry for 2-3 minutes until golden brown and crispy. Remove with a slotted spoon and drain on paper towels.
2. Assemble the Tacos:
    - Warm the tortillas in a skillet or microwave until soft and pliable.

- Place a spoonful of shredded cabbage or lettuce on each tortilla.
- Add a few pieces of tempura shrimp onto the lettuce.
- Top with sliced avocado, sliced cucumber, and thinly sliced radishes.
- Drizzle with sriracha mayo or spicy mayo for a kick of flavor.

3. Serve and Enjoy:
    - Serve the Japanese Tempura Shrimp Tacos immediately, with lime wedges on the side for squeezing over the tacos.
    - Drizzle with soy sauce or ponzu sauce for added umami flavor.
    - Enjoy the light and crispy goodness of tempura shrimp combined with the freshness of taco toppings! Adjust the toppings according to your preference.

Thai Peanut Chicken Tacos

Ingredients:

For the Thai Peanut Chicken:

- 1 lb chicken breast, thinly sliced
- 2 tablespoons vegetable oil
- 1/4 cup Thai peanut sauce
- 2 tablespoons soy sauce
- 1 tablespoon lime juice
- 1 tablespoon honey or brown sugar
- 2 cloves garlic, minced
- 1 teaspoon grated ginger
- Salt and pepper, to taste
- Chopped cilantro, for garnish
- Crushed peanuts, for garnish

For assembling tacos:

- 8-10 small flour or corn tortillas
- Shredded lettuce or cabbage
- Sliced bell peppers
- Sliced red onion
- Sliced cucumber
- Lime wedges, for serving

Instructions:

1. Prepare the Thai Peanut Chicken:
    - In a bowl, whisk together Thai peanut sauce, soy sauce, lime juice, honey or brown sugar, minced garlic, and grated ginger to make the marinade.
    - Add the thinly sliced chicken to the marinade, ensuring it is well coated. Let it marinate for at least 30 minutes.
    - Heat vegetable oil in a skillet over medium-high heat. Add the marinated chicken and cook for 5-7 minutes until cooked through and slightly caramelized. Remove from heat.
2. Assemble the Tacos:

- Warm the tortillas in a skillet or microwave until soft and pliable.
- Place a spoonful of shredded lettuce or cabbage on each tortilla.
- Add a few pieces of Thai Peanut Chicken onto the lettuce.
- Top with sliced bell peppers, sliced red onion, and sliced cucumber.

3. Serve and Enjoy:
    - Serve the Thai Peanut Chicken Tacos immediately, garnished with chopped cilantro and crushed peanuts.
    - Serve with lime wedges on the side for squeezing over the tacos.
    - Enjoy the creamy and flavorful Thai peanut sauce combined with the freshness of taco toppings! Adjust the toppings according to your preference.

Chinese Orange Beef Tacos

Ingredients:

For the Orange Beef:

- 1 lb beef sirloin or flank steak, thinly sliced
- 2 tablespoons vegetable oil
- 2 cloves garlic, minced
- 1 tablespoon grated ginger
- Zest of 1 orange
- 1/4 cup orange juice
- 2 tablespoons soy sauce
- 2 tablespoons hoisin sauce
- 1 tablespoon rice vinegar
- 1 tablespoon brown sugar
- 1 teaspoon cornstarch
- Salt and pepper to taste

For assembling tacos:

- 8-10 small flour or corn tortillas
- Shredded cabbage or lettuce
- Sliced bell peppers
- Sliced green onions
- Orange slices for garnish
- Sesame seeds for garnish
- Sriracha or chili flakes for extra heat (optional)

Instructions:

1. Prepare the Orange Beef:
    - In a bowl, combine orange zest, orange juice, soy sauce, hoisin sauce, rice vinegar, brown sugar, and cornstarch. Mix well to make the sauce.
    - Heat vegetable oil in a skillet over medium-high heat. Add minced garlic and grated ginger. Sauté for 1-2 minutes until fragrant.
    - Add thinly sliced beef to the skillet. Cook until browned on all sides.
    - Pour the orange sauce over the beef. Stir well to coat the beef evenly. Cook for an additional 2-3 minutes until the sauce thickens and beef is cooked through. Remove from heat.

2. Assemble the Tacos:
    - Warm the tortillas in a skillet or microwave until soft and pliable.
    - Place a spoonful of shredded cabbage or lettuce on each tortilla.
    - Add a portion of the orange beef onto the lettuce.
    - Top with sliced bell peppers and sliced green onions.
    - Garnish with orange slices and sesame seeds.
3. Serve and Enjoy:
    - Serve the Chinese Orange Beef Tacos immediately, with sriracha or chili flakes on the side for extra heat if desired.
    - Enjoy the tangy sweetness of orange beef combined with the crunchy freshness of taco toppings! Adjust the toppings and spice level according to your preference.

Vietnamese Pho Beef Tacos

Ingredients:

For the Pho Beef:

- 1 lb beef sirloin or flank steak, thinly sliced
- 4 cups beef broth
- 2 cloves garlic, minced
- 1 onion, thinly sliced
- 1-inch piece of ginger, sliced
- 2 star anise
- 1 cinnamon stick
- 2 tablespoons soy sauce
- 1 tablespoon fish sauce
- 1 tablespoon brown sugar
- Salt and pepper to taste
- Fresh cilantro leaves, for garnish
- Thinly sliced green onions, for garnish
- Bean sprouts, for garnish
- Lime wedges, for serving

For assembling tacos:

- 8-10 small flour or corn tortillas
- Cooked rice noodles or vermicelli
- Thinly sliced cucumber
- Thinly sliced jalapenos
- Thai basil leaves
- Hoisin sauce and sriracha, for topping

Instructions:

1. Prepare the Pho Beef:
    - In a large pot, combine beef broth, minced garlic, sliced onion, sliced ginger, star anise, and cinnamon stick. Bring to a boil.
    - Reduce heat to low and simmer for 20-30 minutes to allow the flavors to meld.
    - Strain the broth and discard the solids. Return the broth to the pot.

- Add thinly sliced beef, soy sauce, fish sauce, and brown sugar to the broth. Simmer for another 5-10 minutes until the beef is cooked through. Season with salt and pepper to taste.
2. Assemble the Tacos:
    - Warm the tortillas in a skillet or microwave until soft and pliable.
    - Place a spoonful of cooked rice noodles or vermicelli on each tortilla.
    - Add a few slices of the cooked pho beef onto the noodles.
    - Top with thinly sliced cucumber, thinly sliced jalapenos, and Thai basil leaves.
3. Serve and Enjoy:
    - Serve the Vietnamese Pho Beef Tacos immediately, with fresh cilantro leaves, thinly sliced green onions, bean sprouts, lime wedges, hoisin sauce, and sriracha on the side.
    - Let your guests customize their tacos with their favorite toppings.
    - Enjoy the rich and aromatic flavors of pho beef in a convenient taco form! Adjust the toppings according to your preference.

Indian Curry Lamb Tacos

Ingredients:

For the Curry Lamb:

- 1 lb ground lamb
- 2 tablespoons vegetable oil
- 1 onion, finely chopped
- 3 cloves garlic, minced
- 1 tablespoon grated ginger
- 2 tablespoons curry powder
- 1 teaspoon ground cumin
- 1 teaspoon ground coriander
- 1/2 teaspoon turmeric powder
- 1/2 teaspoon chili powder (adjust to taste)
- 1/2 cup tomato puree
- Salt and pepper to taste
- Fresh cilantro leaves, chopped for garnish

For assembling tacos:

- 8-10 small flour or corn tortillas
- Shredded lettuce or cabbage
- Diced tomatoes
- Sliced red onion
- Plain yogurt or raita, for topping
- Fresh lime wedges, for serving

Instructions:

1. Prepare the Curry Lamb:
    - Heat vegetable oil in a skillet over medium heat. Add chopped onion and sauté until translucent.
    - Add minced garlic and grated ginger to the skillet. Cook for another minute until fragrant.
    - Add ground lamb to the skillet. Cook until browned, breaking it up with a spoon.
    - Stir in curry powder, ground cumin, ground coriander, turmeric powder, and chili powder. Cook for a couple of minutes until the spices are fragrant.
    - Add tomato puree to the skillet. Stir well to combine.

- Simmer the lamb curry for 10-15 minutes, stirring occasionally, until the flavors meld and the sauce thickens. Season with salt and pepper to taste.
2. Assemble the Tacos:
    - Warm the tortillas in a skillet or microwave until soft and pliable.
    - Place a spoonful of shredded lettuce or cabbage on each tortilla.
    - Add a generous portion of the curry lamb onto the lettuce.
    - Top with diced tomatoes and sliced red onion.
    - Drizzle with plain yogurt or raita for a cool contrast to the spicy curry.
3. Serve and Enjoy:
    - Serve the Indian Curry Lamb Tacos immediately, garnished with chopped cilantro leaves and accompanied by fresh lime wedges.
    - Enjoy the aromatic flavors of Indian curry infused into a taco format! Adjust the spiciness of the curry according to your preference, and feel free to customize the toppings.

Malaysian Nasi Lemak Tacos

Ingredients:

For the Coconut Rice:

- 1 cup jasmine rice
- 1 cup coconut milk
- 1 cup water
- 1 pandan leaf (optional)
- Salt to taste

For the Sambal Sauce:

- 4 tablespoons sambal oelek or Malaysian chili paste
- 2 tablespoons brown sugar
- 1 tablespoon tamarind paste
- 1 tablespoon water
- Salt to taste

For the Toppings:

- Fried anchovies (ikan bilis), drained
- Fried peanuts
- Sliced cucumber
- Sliced hard-boiled eggs
- Fresh cilantro leaves
- Lime wedges

For assembling tacos:

- 8-10 small flour or corn tortillas
- Shredded lettuce or cabbage (optional)

Instructions:

1. Prepare the Coconut Rice:

- Rinse the jasmine rice under cold water until the water runs clear. Drain well.
- In a saucepan, combine the rinsed rice, coconut milk, water, pandan leaf (if using), and a pinch of salt.
- Bring the mixture to a boil, then reduce the heat to low. Cover and simmer for 15-20 minutes, or until the rice is cooked and has absorbed all the liquid. Fluff the rice with a fork and set aside.

2. Make the Sambal Sauce:
   - In a small saucepan, combine the sambal oelek, brown sugar, tamarind paste, water, and a pinch of salt.
   - Cook over low heat, stirring constantly, until the sauce thickens slightly and the sugar has dissolved. Remove from heat and set aside.
3. Assemble the Tacos:
   - Warm the tortillas in a skillet or microwave until soft and pliable.
   - Spread a spoonful of coconut rice onto each tortilla.
   - Top the rice with a spoonful of sambal sauce.
   - Add a few fried anchovies, fried peanuts, sliced cucumber, and sliced hard-boiled eggs on top.
   - Garnish with fresh cilantro leaves and serve with lime wedges on the side.
4. Serve and Enjoy:
   - Serve the Malaysian Nasi Lemak Tacos immediately, allowing your guests to customize their tacos with additional toppings as desired.
   - Enjoy the unique combination of flavors and textures reminiscent of the beloved Malaysian dish, Nasi Lemak, in a fun and portable taco form! Adjust the spice level and toppings according to your preference.

Korean Dak Galbi Chicken Tacos

Ingredients:

For the Dak Galbi Chicken:

- 1 lb boneless chicken thighs, cut into bite-sized pieces
- 2 tablespoons Korean chili paste (gochujang)
- 1 tablespoon soy sauce
- 1 tablespoon rice wine (mirin)
- 1 tablespoon honey or brown sugar
- 2 cloves garlic, minced
- 1 tablespoon vegetable oil
- 1 onion, sliced
- 1 carrot, julienned
- 1/2 cabbage, thinly sliced
- 2 green onions, chopped
- Salt and pepper to taste

For assembling tacos:

- 8-10 small flour or corn tortillas
- Shredded lettuce or cabbage
- Sliced cucumber
- Sliced radishes
- Kimchi, for topping
- Sesame seeds, for garnish
- Lime wedges, for serving

Instructions:

1. Prepare the Dak Galbi Chicken:
    - In a bowl, combine Korean chili paste, soy sauce, rice wine, honey or brown sugar, and minced garlic to make the marinade.
    - Add the chicken pieces to the marinade, ensuring they are well coated. Let it marinate for at least 30 minutes.
    - Heat vegetable oil in a skillet or wok over medium-high heat. Add sliced onion and julienned carrot. Stir-fry for a few minutes until softened.
    - Add the marinated chicken to the skillet. Cook until the chicken is no longer pink and has caramelized edges.

- Stir in the thinly sliced cabbage and chopped green onions. Cook until the cabbage is wilted but still slightly crunchy. Season with salt and pepper to taste.

2. Assemble the Tacos:
    - Warm the tortillas in a skillet or microwave until soft and pliable.
    - Place a spoonful of shredded lettuce or cabbage on each tortilla.
    - Add a portion of the Dak Galbi Chicken onto the lettuce.
    - Top with sliced cucumber, sliced radishes, and kimchi for extra flavor and crunch.
3. Serve and Enjoy:
    - Garnish the Korean Dak Galbi Chicken Tacos with sesame seeds and serve with lime wedges on the side.
    - Serve immediately and enjoy the spicy and savory flavors of Dak Galbi in a taco format! Adjust the toppings according to your preference and spice level.

Thai Coconut Curry Shrimp Tacos

Ingredients:

For the Coconut Curry Shrimp:

- 1 lb large shrimp, peeled and deveined
- 2 tablespoons red curry paste
- 1 can (13.5 oz) coconut milk
- 2 tablespoons fish sauce
- 1 tablespoon brown sugar
- 1 red bell pepper, thinly sliced
- 1 cup sliced mushrooms
- 1 tablespoon vegetable oil
- Salt and pepper to taste
- Fresh cilantro leaves for garnish

For assembling tacos:

- 8-10 small flour or corn tortillas
- Shredded cabbage or lettuce
- Sliced avocado
- Sliced red onion
- Lime wedges for serving

Instructions:

1. Prepare the Coconut Curry Shrimp:
    - In a large skillet, heat vegetable oil over medium heat. Add red curry paste and cook for 1-2 minutes until fragrant.
    - Stir in coconut milk, fish sauce, and brown sugar. Bring to a simmer.
    - Add sliced red bell pepper and mushrooms to the skillet. Cook for 2-3 minutes until slightly softened.
    - Add the peeled and deveined shrimp to the skillet. Cook for 3-4 minutes until the shrimp are pink and cooked through. Season with salt and pepper to taste.
2. Assemble the Tacos:
    - Warm the tortillas in a skillet or microwave until soft and pliable.

- Place a spoonful of shredded cabbage or lettuce on each tortilla.
- Add a few spoonfuls of the coconut curry shrimp onto the cabbage.
- Top with sliced avocado and sliced red onion.
3. Serve and Enjoy:
    - Garnish the Thai Coconut Curry Shrimp Tacos with fresh cilantro leaves and serve with lime wedges on the side.
    - Serve immediately and enjoy the creamy and aromatic flavors of Thai coconut curry combined with succulent shrimp in a taco format! Adjust the toppings according to your preference.

Japanese Tonkatsu Pork Tacos

Ingredients:

For the Tonkatsu Pork:

- 4 boneless pork loin chops, about 1/2 inch thick
- Salt and pepper
- 1/2 cup all-purpose flour
- 2 large eggs, beaten
- 1 cup panko breadcrumbs
- Vegetable oil, for frying

For the Tonkatsu Sauce:

- 1/4 cup ketchup
- 2 tablespoons Worcestershire sauce
- 1 tablespoon soy sauce
- 1 tablespoon rice vinegar
- 1 tablespoon sugar

For assembling tacos:

- 8-10 small flour or corn tortillas
- Shredded cabbage or lettuce
- Sliced cucumber
- Sliced tomatoes
- Thinly sliced green onions
- Japanese mayonnaise (optional)
- Pickled ginger (optional)
- Lime wedges, for serving

Instructions:

1. Prepare the Tonkatsu Pork:
    - Season the pork chops with salt and pepper on both sides.
    - Set up a breading station with three shallow bowls: one with flour, one with beaten eggs, and one with panko breadcrumbs.

- Dredge each pork chop in the flour, shaking off any excess. Dip into the beaten eggs, then coat with panko breadcrumbs, pressing gently to adhere.
- Heat vegetable oil in a large skillet over medium-high heat. Fry the breaded pork chops for 3-4 minutes on each side, or until golden brown and cooked through. Transfer to a paper towel-lined plate to drain.

2. Make the Tonkatsu Sauce:
    - In a small saucepan, combine ketchup, Worcestershire sauce, soy sauce, rice vinegar, and sugar. Cook over medium heat, stirring constantly, until the sugar is dissolved and the sauce has thickened slightly. Remove from heat and set aside.
3. Assemble the Tacos:
    - Warm the tortillas in a skillet or microwave until soft and pliable.
    - Place a spoonful of shredded cabbage or lettuce on each tortilla.
    - Slice the tonkatsu pork chops into strips and place on top of the cabbage.
    - Add sliced cucumber, sliced tomatoes, and thinly sliced green onions.
    - Drizzle with tonkatsu sauce and Japanese mayonnaise, if desired. Top with pickled ginger for an extra kick of flavor.
4. Serve and Enjoy:
    - Serve the Japanese Tonkatsu Pork Tacos immediately, with lime wedges on the side for squeezing over the tacos.
    - Enjoy the crispy and flavorful tonkatsu pork combined with fresh taco toppings! Adjust the toppings according to your preference.

Filipino Adobo Chicken Tacos

Ingredients:

For the Adobo Chicken:

- 1 lb boneless, skinless chicken thighs
- 1/2 cup soy sauce
- 1/2 cup vinegar (preferably cane or apple cider vinegar)
- 4 cloves garlic, minced
- 1 bay leaf
- 1 teaspoon whole peppercorns
- 1 tablespoon vegetable oil

For assembling tacos:

- 8-10 small flour or corn tortillas
- Shredded lettuce or cabbage
- Sliced tomatoes
- Sliced red onions
- Chopped fresh cilantro (optional)
- Lime wedges, for serving

Instructions:

1. Prepare the Adobo Chicken:
    - In a bowl, combine soy sauce, vinegar, minced garlic, bay leaf, and whole peppercorns to make the adobo marinade.
    - Add the chicken thighs to the marinade, ensuring they are well coated. Marinate in the refrigerator for at least 1 hour, or preferably overnight for maximum flavor.
    - Heat vegetable oil in a skillet over medium-high heat. Remove the chicken from the marinade and pat dry with paper towels.
    - Add the chicken to the skillet and cook for 5-6 minutes on each side, or until browned and cooked through. Remove from the skillet and let it rest for a few minutes before slicing.
2. Assemble the Tacos:
    - Warm the tortillas in a skillet or microwave until soft and pliable.
    - Place a spoonful of shredded lettuce or cabbage on each tortilla.
    - Add slices of cooked adobo chicken onto the lettuce.
    - Top with sliced tomatoes and sliced red onions.

- Sprinkle with chopped fresh cilantro, if desired.
3. Serve and Enjoy:
    - Serve the Filipino Adobo Chicken Tacos immediately, with lime wedges on the side for squeezing over the tacos.
    - Enjoy the savory and tangy flavors of Filipino adobo combined with fresh taco toppings! Adjust the toppings according to your preference.

Chinese Sweet and Sour Tofu Tacos

Ingredients:

For the Sweet and Sour Tofu:

- 1 block (14 oz) firm tofu, drained and pressed
- 2 tablespoons cornstarch
- 2 tablespoons vegetable oil
- 1 bell pepper, diced
- 1 onion, diced
- 1 cup pineapple chunks
- 1/4 cup ketchup
- 2 tablespoons rice vinegar
- 2 tablespoons soy sauce
- 2 tablespoons brown sugar
- 1 teaspoon grated ginger
- 1 clove garlic, minced
- Salt and pepper to taste

For assembling tacos:

- 8-10 small flour or corn tortillas
- Shredded lettuce or cabbage
- Sliced cucumber
- Sliced green onions
- Sesame seeds for garnish
- Lime wedges for serving

Instructions:

1. Prepare the Sweet and Sour Tofu:
    - Cut the pressed tofu into cubes and toss them in cornstarch until evenly coated.
    - Heat vegetable oil in a large skillet over medium-high heat. Add the tofu cubes and cook until golden and crispy on all sides. Remove from the skillet and set aside.
    - In the same skillet, add diced bell pepper and onion. Cook until softened, about 3-4 minutes.
    - Stir in pineapple chunks and cook for another 2 minutes.

- In a small bowl, whisk together ketchup, rice vinegar, soy sauce, brown sugar, grated ginger, minced garlic, salt, and pepper. Pour the sauce over the vegetables in the skillet.
- Return the crispy tofu cubes to the skillet and toss everything together until well coated in the sweet and sour sauce. Cook for an additional 2-3 minutes until heated through.

2. Assemble the Tacos:
    - Warm the tortillas in a skillet or microwave until soft and pliable.
    - Place a spoonful of shredded lettuce or cabbage on each tortilla.
    - Add a portion of the sweet and sour tofu mixture onto the lettuce.
    - Top with sliced cucumber and sliced green onions.
3. Serve and Enjoy:
    - Garnish the Chinese Sweet and Sour Tofu Tacos with sesame seeds and serve with lime wedges on the side.
    - Serve immediately and enjoy the tangy sweetness of the tofu combined with fresh taco toppings! Adjust the toppings according to your preference.

Indian Tikka Masala Tofu Tacos

Ingredients:

For the Tikka Masala Tofu:

- 1 block (14 oz) firm tofu, drained and pressed
- 2 tablespoons tikka masala paste or powder
- 1/4 cup plain yogurt
- 2 tablespoons vegetable oil
- 1 onion, finely chopped
- 2 cloves garlic, minced
- 1-inch piece of ginger, grated
- 1 can (14 oz) diced tomatoes
- 1/2 cup coconut milk
- Salt and pepper to taste
- Fresh cilantro leaves for garnish

For assembling tacos:

- 8-10 small flour or corn tortillas
- Shredded lettuce or cabbage
- Sliced cucumber
- Sliced red onion
- Plain yogurt or raita, for topping
- Lime wedges, for serving

Instructions:

1. Prepare the Tikka Masala Tofu:
    - Cut the pressed tofu into cubes and place them in a bowl.
    - In another bowl, mix tikka masala paste or powder with plain yogurt to form a marinade. Pour the marinade over the tofu cubes and toss until well coated. Let it marinate for at least 30 minutes.
    - Heat vegetable oil in a large skillet over medium-high heat. Add marinated tofu cubes and cook until browned on all sides. Remove tofu from the skillet and set aside.

- In the same skillet, add chopped onion and cook until softened, about 5 minutes. Stir in minced garlic and grated ginger, and cook for another minute.
- Add diced tomatoes (with their juices) to the skillet. Cook until the tomatoes break down and the sauce thickens slightly.
- Stir in coconut milk and cooked tofu cubes. Simmer for 5-10 minutes, until the tofu is heated through and the sauce is flavorful. Season with salt and pepper to taste.

2. Assemble the Tacos:
    - Warm the tortillas in a skillet or microwave until soft and pliable.
    - Place a spoonful of shredded lettuce or cabbage on each tortilla.
    - Add a portion of the tikka masala tofu mixture onto the lettuce.
    - Top with sliced cucumber and sliced red onion.
    - Drizzle with plain yogurt or raita for a cool contrast to the spicy tikka masala.

3. Serve and Enjoy:
    - Garnish the Indian Tikka Masala Tofu Tacos with fresh cilantro leaves and serve with lime wedges on the side.
    - Serve immediately and enjoy the rich and aromatic flavors of tikka masala combined with fresh taco toppings! Adjust the toppings according to your preference.

Malaysian Rendang Chicken Tacos

Ingredients:

For the Rendang Chicken:

- 1 lb boneless, skinless chicken thighs, cut into bite-sized pieces
- 2 tablespoons vegetable oil
- 1 onion, finely chopped
- 3 cloves garlic, minced
- 1-inch piece of ginger, grated
- 2 tablespoons Malaysian rendang curry paste
- 1 can (14 oz) coconut milk
- 1 cinnamon stick
- 2 cardamom pods
- 2 tablespoons brown sugar
- Salt to taste

For assembling tacos:

- 8-10 small flour or corn tortillas
- Shredded lettuce or cabbage
- Sliced cucumber
- Sliced red onion
- Fresh cilantro leaves for garnish
- Lime wedges for serving

Instructions:

1. Prepare the Rendang Chicken:
    - Heat vegetable oil in a large skillet over medium heat. Add chopped onion and cook until softened, about 5 minutes.
    - Stir in minced garlic and grated ginger, and cook for another minute until fragrant.
    - Add Malaysian rendang curry paste to the skillet and cook for 2-3 minutes, stirring constantly.
    - Add chicken pieces to the skillet and cook until browned on all sides.
    - Pour in coconut milk and add cinnamon stick and cardamom pods. Stir to combine.
    - Bring the mixture to a simmer, then reduce heat to low. Cover and let it simmer for 30-40 minutes, stirring occasionally, until the chicken is tender and the sauce has thickened.

- Stir in brown sugar and season with salt to taste.
2. Assemble the Tacos:
    - Warm the tortillas in a skillet or microwave until soft and pliable.
    - Place a spoonful of shredded lettuce or cabbage on each tortilla.
    - Add a portion of the rendang chicken onto the lettuce.
    - Top with sliced cucumber and sliced red onion.
3. Serve and Enjoy:
    - Garnish the Malaysian Rendang Chicken Tacos with fresh cilantro leaves and serve with lime wedges on the side.
    - Serve immediately and enjoy the rich and aromatic flavors of Malaysian rendang combined with fresh taco toppings! Adjust the toppings according to your preference.

Korean Japchae Beef Tacos

Ingredients:

For the Japchae Beef:

- 1 lb beef sirloin, thinly sliced
- 4 tablespoons soy sauce
- 2 tablespoons sesame oil
- 2 tablespoons brown sugar
- 2 cloves garlic, minced
- 1 teaspoon grated ginger
- 1 onion, thinly sliced
- 1 carrot, julienned
- 1 red bell pepper, thinly sliced
- 4 ounces dried Korean sweet potato starch noodles (dangmyeon)
- 2 green onions, thinly sliced
- Toasted sesame seeds for garnish
- Cooking oil

For assembling tacos:

- 8-10 small flour or corn tortillas
- Shredded lettuce or cabbage
- Sliced cucumber
- Sliced radishes
- Gochujang (Korean chili paste), for topping (optional)
- Lime wedges, for serving

Instructions:

1. Prepare the Japchae Beef:
    - In a bowl, combine thinly sliced beef with soy sauce, sesame oil, brown sugar, minced garlic, and grated ginger. Let it marinate for at least 30 minutes.
    - Meanwhile, cook the sweet potato starch noodles according to the package instructions until they are soft but still chewy. Drain and rinse under cold water to stop the cooking process. Set aside.
    - Heat some cooking oil in a large skillet or wok over medium-high heat. Add the marinated beef slices and stir-fry until cooked through. Remove the beef from the skillet and set aside.

- In the same skillet, add a bit more oil if needed and stir-fry the sliced onion, julienned carrot, and thinly sliced red bell pepper until softened.
- Add the cooked noodles and sliced green onions to the skillet. Stir-fry everything together for a few minutes until well combined and heated through.
- Return the cooked beef to the skillet and toss everything together until evenly mixed. Remove from heat.
2. Assemble the Tacos:
    - Warm the tortillas in a skillet or microwave until soft and pliable.
    - Place a spoonful of shredded lettuce or cabbage on each tortilla.
    - Add a portion of the japchae beef mixture onto the lettuce.
    - Top with sliced cucumber and sliced radishes.
3. Serve and Enjoy:
    - Garnish the Korean Japchae Beef Tacos with toasted sesame seeds and serve with lime wedges on the side.
    - For an extra kick of flavor, drizzle with gochujang (Korean chili paste) if desired.
    - Serve immediately and enjoy the savory and sweet flavors of Korean japchae in taco form! Adjust the toppings according to your preference.

Thai Mango Sticky Rice Tacos

Ingredients:

- 1 cup glutinous rice (also known as sticky rice)
- 1 cup coconut milk
- 1/2 cup sugar
- 1/2 teaspoon salt
- 2 ripe mangoes, peeled and sliced
- 8 small soft taco shells or tortillas
- Optional garnishes: toasted sesame seeds, shredded coconut, mint leaves

Instructions:

1. Prepare the Sticky Rice:
    - Rinse the glutinous rice under cold water until the water runs clear.
    - Soak the rice in water for at least 1 hour, or preferably overnight.
    - Drain the rice and place it in a steamer lined with cheesecloth. Steam the rice over medium heat for about 25-30 minutes, or until cooked through and tender.
2. Make the Coconut Sauce:
    - In a saucepan, combine the coconut milk, sugar, and salt. Heat over medium heat, stirring occasionally, until the sugar is dissolved and the mixture is heated through. Do not boil.
    - Once the rice is cooked, transfer it to a large bowl and pour the coconut sauce over it. Mix well until the rice is evenly coated with the sauce. Let it cool slightly.
3. Assemble the Tacos:
    - Warm the taco shells or tortillas according to package instructions.
    - Spoon a generous amount of the sticky rice onto each taco shell.
    - Top with sliced mangoes and any optional garnishes you desire, such as toasted sesame seeds, shredded coconut, or mint leaves.
4. Serve:
    - Serve the Thai Mango Sticky Rice Tacos immediately, while the rice is still warm and the flavors are fresh.

Enjoy the delightful blend of flavors and textures in these Thai-inspired tacos!

Japanese Okonomiyaki Tacos

Ingredients:

For Okonomiyaki Batter:

- 2 cups shredded cabbage
- 1 cup all-purpose flour
- 3/4 cup dashi stock (or substitute with water or chicken/vegetable broth)
- 2 large eggs
- 2 green onions, thinly sliced
- 1/4 cup tenkasu (tempura scraps)
- 1/4 cup chopped cooked shrimp or bacon (optional)
- Salt and pepper to taste

For Toppings:

- Okonomiyaki sauce (store-bought or homemade, see below)
- Japanese mayonnaise
- Thinly sliced green onions
- Bonito flakes (katsuobushi)
- Nori (seaweed), thinly sliced

For Taco Assembly:

- 8 small soft taco shells or tortillas

Instructions:

1. Prepare the Okonomiyaki Batter:
    - In a large bowl, combine shredded cabbage, flour, dashi stock, eggs, green onions, tenkasu, and cooked shrimp or bacon (if using). Season with salt and pepper. Mix until well combined.
2. Cook the Okonomiyaki:
    - Heat a non-stick skillet or griddle over medium heat. Lightly oil the surface.
    - Pour about 1/2 cup of the batter onto the skillet, spreading it into a circle about the size of a small tortilla. Cook for 3-4 minutes on each side, or until golden brown and cooked through. Repeat with the remaining batter.
3. Make the Okonomiyaki Sauce:
    - In a small bowl, mix together 1/4 cup ketchup, 2 tablespoons Worcestershire sauce, 1 tablespoon soy sauce, and 1 tablespoon honey. Adjust the proportions to your taste.
4. Assemble the Tacos:

- Place one okonomiyaki pancake on each taco shell.
- Drizzle with okonomiyaki sauce and Japanese mayonnaise.
- Sprinkle with sliced green onions, bonito flakes, and nori strips.
5. Serve:
    - Serve the Japanese Okonomiyaki Tacos immediately, while the okonomiyaki is warm and the toppings are fresh.

Enjoy the unique fusion of flavors in these Japanese-inspired tacos! They're perfect for a fun and tasty meal.

Vietnamese Caramelized Pork Belly Tacos

Ingredients:

For Caramelized Pork Belly:

- 1 lb pork belly, thinly sliced
- 3 cloves garlic, minced
- 2 tablespoons fish sauce
- 2 tablespoons soy sauce
- 2 tablespoons sugar
- 1 tablespoon vegetable oil
- 1/4 teaspoon black pepper

For Tacos:

- 8 small soft taco shells or tortillas
- Thinly sliced cucumber
- Thinly sliced carrots
- Fresh cilantro leaves
- Fresh mint leaves
- Fresh basil leaves
- Lime wedges, for serving

Instructions:

1. Marinate the Pork Belly:
    - In a bowl, combine the thinly sliced pork belly with minced garlic, fish sauce, soy sauce, sugar, and black pepper. Mix well to ensure the pork is evenly coated. Let it marinate for at least 30 minutes, or overnight for best results.
2. Caramelize the Pork Belly:
    - Heat vegetable oil in a skillet over medium-high heat.
    - Add the marinated pork belly slices to the skillet, spreading them out in a single layer. Cook for 3-4 minutes on each side, or until caramelized and cooked through. Remove from the skillet and set aside.
3. Prepare the Toppings:
    - Thinly slice cucumber and carrots. Wash and dry fresh cilantro, mint, and basil leaves.

4. Assemble the Tacos:
    - Warm the taco shells or tortillas according to package instructions.
    - Place a few slices of caramelized pork belly onto each taco shell.
    - Top with sliced cucumber, carrots, and a generous handful of fresh cilantro, mint, and basil leaves.
5. Serve:
    - Serve the Vietnamese Caramelized Pork Belly Tacos with lime wedges on the side for squeezing over the tacos.

Enjoy the delicious combination of savory caramelized pork belly with fresh herbs and vegetables in these Vietnamese-inspired tacos!

Indian Vindaloo Beef Tacos

Ingredients:

For Vindaloo Beef:

- 1 lb beef, thinly sliced (such as sirloin or flank steak)
- 3 tablespoons vindaloo paste (store-bought or homemade)
- 2 tablespoons vegetable oil
- 1 onion, thinly sliced
- 3 cloves garlic, minced
- 1-inch piece of ginger, grated
- 1 teaspoon ground cumin
- 1 teaspoon ground coriander
- 1/2 teaspoon turmeric powder
- Salt and pepper to taste
- 1/2 cup beef or vegetable broth

For Tacos:

- 8 small soft taco shells or tortillas
- Finely shredded lettuce
- Diced tomatoes
- Chopped cilantro
- Greek yogurt or sour cream, for serving
- Lime wedges, for serving

Instructions:

1. Marinate the Beef:
    - In a bowl, combine the thinly sliced beef with vindaloo paste. Mix well to ensure the beef is evenly coated. Let it marinate for at least 30 minutes, or longer if time allows.
2. Cook the Vindaloo Beef:
    - Heat vegetable oil in a skillet over medium-high heat.
    - Add the sliced onion to the skillet and sauté until softened, about 3-4 minutes.
    - Add minced garlic and grated ginger to the skillet, and cook for another 1-2 minutes until fragrant.

- Add the marinated beef to the skillet, spreading it out in a single layer. Cook for 3-4 minutes, stirring occasionally, until the beef is browned.
- Stir in ground cumin, ground coriander, turmeric powder, salt, and pepper. Cook for another 1-2 minutes.
- Pour in beef or vegetable broth, scraping any browned bits from the bottom of the skillet. Reduce heat to low and simmer for 5-7 minutes, or until the beef is cooked through and the sauce has thickened slightly.

3. Assemble the Tacos:
   - Warm the taco shells or tortillas according to package instructions.
   - Place a spoonful of vindaloo beef onto each taco shell.
   - Top with finely shredded lettuce, diced tomatoes, and chopped cilantro.
   - Serve with Greek yogurt or sour cream on the side for dolloping over the tacos.
4. Serve:
   - Serve the Indian Vindaloo Beef Tacos with lime wedges on the side for squeezing over the tacos.

Enjoy the spicy and flavorful twist of Indian vindaloo beef in these delicious tacos!

Malaysian Laksa Shrimp Tacos

Ingredients:

For Laksa Shrimp:

- 1 lb large shrimp, peeled and deveined
- 2 tablespoons laksa paste (store-bought or homemade)
- 1 can (14 oz) coconut milk
- 2 cups chicken or vegetable broth
- 1 tablespoon fish sauce
- 1 tablespoon brown sugar
- Juice of 1 lime
- Salt to taste
- Chopped cilantro, for garnish

For Tacos:

- 8 small soft taco shells or tortillas
- Thinly sliced cucumber
- Thinly sliced red onion
- Bean sprouts
- Fresh cilantro leaves
- Lime wedges, for serving

Instructions:

1. Prepare Laksa Shrimp:
    - In a large skillet or pot, heat laksa paste over medium heat for 1-2 minutes until fragrant.
    - Stir in coconut milk and chicken or vegetable broth. Bring to a simmer.
    - Add fish sauce, brown sugar, and lime juice. Stir to combine.
    - Add shrimp to the skillet and cook for 3-4 minutes, or until shrimp are pink and cooked through.
    - Season with salt to taste. Garnish with chopped cilantro.
2. Assemble the Tacos:
    - Warm the taco shells or tortillas according to package instructions.
    - Place a spoonful of laksa shrimp onto each taco shell.
    - Top with thinly sliced cucumber, red onion, bean sprouts, and fresh cilantro leaves.
3. Serve:
    - Serve the Malaysian Laksa Shrimp Tacos with lime wedges on the side for squeezing over the tacos.

These tacos offer a delightful fusion of Malaysian flavors with the convenience of handheld tacos. Enjoy the bold and aromatic taste of laksa with juicy shrimp in every bite!

Korean Dak Bulgogi Tacos

Ingredients:

For Dak Bulgogi (Marinated Chicken):

- 1 lb boneless, skinless chicken thighs, thinly sliced
- 3 tablespoons soy sauce
- 2 tablespoons brown sugar
- 1 tablespoon sesame oil
- 3 cloves garlic, minced
- 1 teaspoon ginger, grated
- 1 tablespoon rice vinegar
- 1 tablespoon gochujang (Korean red pepper paste)
- 2 green onions, chopped
- 1 tablespoon vegetable oil, for cooking

For Tacos:

- 8 small soft taco shells or tortillas
- Shredded lettuce
- Thinly sliced red cabbage
- Thinly sliced cucumber
- Kimchi (optional)
- Sesame seeds, for garnish
- Sliced green onions, for garnish
- Sriracha mayo or Korean gochujang mayo, for serving (optional)

Instructions:

1. Marinate the Chicken:
    - In a bowl, combine soy sauce, brown sugar, sesame oil, minced garlic, grated ginger, rice vinegar, gochujang, and chopped green onions.
    - Add the thinly sliced chicken thighs to the marinade and mix well to coat. Let it marinate for at least 30 minutes, or up to overnight in the refrigerator.
2. Cook the Dak Bulgogi:
    - Heat vegetable oil in a skillet or grill pan over medium-high heat.

- Add the marinated chicken to the skillet in a single layer. Cook for 3-4 minutes on each side, or until the chicken is cooked through and caramelized.
3. Prepare the Toppings:
    - While the chicken is cooking, prepare the taco toppings. Shred lettuce, thinly slice red cabbage and cucumber. If using, prepare kimchi.
4. Assemble the Tacos:
    - Warm the taco shells or tortillas according to package instructions.
    - Place a spoonful of cooked Dak Bulgogi onto each taco shell.
    - Top with shredded lettuce, sliced red cabbage, cucumber, and kimchi (if using).
    - Garnish with sesame seeds and sliced green onions.
5. Serve:
    - Serve the Korean Dak Bulgogi Tacos with sriracha mayo or Korean gochujang mayo on the side for drizzling over the tacos, if desired.

These tacos offer a delightful blend of spicy, sweet, and savory flavors, perfect for a fusion meal that's sure to impress! Enjoy the Korean twist on this beloved Mexican dish.

Thai Pineapple Fried Rice Tacos

Ingredients:

For Thai Pineapple Fried Rice:

- 2 cups cooked jasmine rice, chilled
- 1 tablespoon vegetable oil
- 2 cloves garlic, minced
- 1 small onion, finely chopped
- 1 red bell pepper, diced
- 1 cup diced pineapple (fresh or canned)
- 1/2 cup frozen peas, thawed
- 2 tablespoons soy sauce
- 1 tablespoon fish sauce
- 1 tablespoon oyster sauce (optional)
- 1 teaspoon curry powder
- Salt and pepper to taste
- Chopped green onions, for garnish
- Chopped cilantro, for garnish
- Lime wedges, for serving

For Tacos:

- 8 small soft taco shells or tortillas

Instructions:

1. Prepare Thai Pineapple Fried Rice:
    - Heat vegetable oil in a large skillet or wok over medium-high heat.
    - Add minced garlic and chopped onion to the skillet. Stir-fry for 1-2 minutes until fragrant and onions are translucent.
    - Add diced red bell pepper and cook for another 2-3 minutes until slightly softened.
    - Stir in diced pineapple and thawed peas. Cook for 2 minutes.
    - Add chilled cooked jasmine rice to the skillet, breaking up any clumps with a spatula.
    - Drizzle soy sauce, fish sauce, and oyster sauce (if using) over the rice. Sprinkle curry powder, salt, and pepper. Stir well to combine.
    - Cook for an additional 3-4 minutes, stirring frequently, until the rice is heated through and evenly coated with the sauce.
    - Remove from heat and garnish with chopped green onions and cilantro.
2. Assemble the Tacos:
    - Warm the taco shells or tortillas according to package instructions.
    - Spoon a generous amount of Thai Pineapple Fried Rice into each taco shell.

3. Serve:
    - Serve the Thai Pineapple Fried Rice Tacos immediately, garnished with lime wedges on the side for squeezing over the tacos.

These Thai-inspired tacos offer a delightful combination of sweet and savory flavors, perfect for a unique and flavorful meal! Enjoy the fusion of Thai Pineapple Fried Rice with the handheld convenience of tacos.

Chinese General Tso's Chicken Tacos

Ingredients:

For General Tso's Chicken:

- 1 lb boneless, skinless chicken thighs, cut into bite-sized pieces
- 1/4 cup cornstarch
- 2 tablespoons vegetable oil, for frying
- 2 cloves garlic, minced
- 1 teaspoon ginger, grated
- 1/2 cup soy sauce
- 1/4 cup hoisin sauce
- 2 tablespoons rice vinegar
- 2 tablespoons brown sugar
- 1 tablespoon cornstarch mixed with 2 tablespoons water (slurry)
- Green onions, chopped, for garnish
- Sesame seeds, for garnish

For Tacos:

- 8 small soft taco shells or tortillas
- Shredded lettuce
- Thinly sliced red bell pepper
- Thinly sliced cucumber
- Sliced green onions, for garnish

Instructions:

1. Prepare General Tso's Chicken:
    - Place chicken pieces in a bowl and toss with cornstarch until evenly coated.
    - Heat vegetable oil in a large skillet or wok over medium-high heat.
    - Add the coated chicken pieces to the skillet in a single layer. Cook for 4-5 minutes on each side, or until golden brown and cooked through. Remove chicken from skillet and set aside.
2. Make General Tso's Sauce:
    - In the same skillet, add minced garlic and grated ginger. Cook for 1-2 minutes until fragrant.

- Add soy sauce, hoisin sauce, rice vinegar, and brown sugar to the skillet. Stir to combine and bring to a simmer.
- Add the cornstarch slurry to the skillet and cook, stirring constantly, until the sauce thickens.

3. Combine Chicken with Sauce:
    - Return the cooked chicken to the skillet with the thickened sauce. Stir until the chicken is evenly coated with the sauce. Cook for an additional 2-3 minutes.
4. Assemble the Tacos:
    - Warm the taco shells or tortillas according to package instructions.
    - Place a spoonful of General Tso's Chicken onto each taco shell.
    - Top with shredded lettuce, sliced red bell pepper, and sliced cucumber.
    - Garnish with chopped green onions and sesame seeds.
5. Serve:
    - Serve the Chinese General Tso's Chicken Tacos immediately, while the chicken is hot and the toppings are fresh.

These tacos offer a delightful blend of sweet, savory, and spicy flavors, perfect for a unique twist on a classic Chinese dish. Enjoy the fusion of General Tso's Chicken with the handheld convenience of tacos!

Filipino Sinigang Fish Tacos

Ingredients:

For Sinigang Fish:

- 1 lb white fish fillets (such as tilapia or cod), cut into bite-sized pieces
- 1 tablespoon vegetable oil
- 1 packet (1.4 oz) sinigang soup mix (available in Asian grocery stores)
- 4 cups water
- 1 small onion, sliced
- 2 tomatoes, quartered
- 1 radish, sliced
- 1 cup green beans, cut into 2-inch pieces
- 2 cups spinach leaves
- Salt to taste
- Fish sauce or patis, to taste (optional)
- Lime wedges, for serving

For Tacos:

- 8 small soft taco shells or tortillas
- Shredded cabbage or lettuce
- Sliced red onion
- Chopped cilantro
- Sliced jalapeños (optional)

Instructions:

1. Prepare Sinigang Fish:
    - In a pot, heat vegetable oil over medium heat. Add sliced onion and cook until translucent.
    - Add sinigang soup mix and water to the pot. Stir well to dissolve the soup mix.
    - Bring the broth to a boil, then reduce heat to simmer.
    - Add quartered tomatoes, sliced radish, and green beans to the pot. Simmer for about 8-10 minutes until the vegetables are tender.
    - Season the broth with salt and fish sauce or patis to taste, if desired.

- Add fish fillet pieces to the pot and simmer for 5-7 minutes until the fish is cooked through.
    - Stir in spinach leaves and cook for another 1-2 minutes until wilted.
2. Assemble the Tacos:
    - Warm the taco shells or tortillas according to package instructions.
    - Place a spoonful of Sinigang Fish onto each taco shell.
    - Top with shredded cabbage or lettuce, sliced red onion, chopped cilantro, and sliced jalapeños if using.
3. Serve:
    - Serve the Filipino Sinigang Fish Tacos immediately, with lime wedges on the side for squeezing over the tacos.

These tacos offer a unique blend of tangy and savory flavors from the Filipino sinigang soup, perfectly complemented by the freshness of the taco toppings. Enjoy the fusion of Filipino and Mexican cuisines in every delicious bite!

Indian Saag Paneer Tacos

Ingredients:

For Saag Paneer:

- 1 lb paneer, cut into cubes
- 2 tablespoons ghee or vegetable oil
- 1 onion, finely chopped
- 3 cloves garlic, minced
- 1-inch piece of ginger, grated
- 2 green chilies, finely chopped (optional)
- 1 teaspoon cumin seeds
- 1 teaspoon ground coriander
- 1/2 teaspoon turmeric powder
- 1/2 teaspoon garam masala
- 1/4 teaspoon cayenne pepper (adjust to taste)
- Salt to taste
- 2 bunches spinach, washed and chopped
- 1/4 cup heavy cream (optional)
- Juice of 1/2 lemon

For Tacos:

- 8 small soft taco shells or tortillas
- Sliced red onions
- Chopped tomatoes
- Chopped cilantro
- Greek yogurt or raita, for serving (optional)

Instructions:

1. Prepare Saag Paneer:
    - Heat ghee or vegetable oil in a large skillet over medium heat.
    - Add chopped onions and sauté until translucent.
    - Add minced garlic, grated ginger, and chopped green chilies (if using). Cook for 1-2 minutes until fragrant.
    - Add cumin seeds, ground coriander, turmeric powder, garam masala, cayenne pepper, and salt. Stir well to combine.
    - Add chopped spinach to the skillet and cook until wilted.
    - Transfer the mixture to a blender or food processor and blend until smooth. Return the mixture to the skillet.
    - Add paneer cubes to the skillet and simmer for 5-7 minutes, stirring occasionally.

- Stir in heavy cream (if using) and lemon juice. Cook for an additional 2-3 minutes.
2. Assemble the Tacos:
    - Warm the taco shells or tortillas according to package instructions.
    - Spoon a generous amount of Saag Paneer onto each taco shell.
    - Top with sliced red onions, chopped tomatoes, and chopped cilantro.
    - Serve with Greek yogurt or raita on the side for drizzling over the tacos, if desired.
3. Serve:
    - Serve the Indian Saag Paneer Tacos immediately, while the Saag Paneer is hot and the toppings are fresh.

These tacos offer a delightful fusion of creamy spinach and tender paneer, perfectly complemented by the fresh taco toppings. Enjoy the Indian-inspired twist on this beloved Mexican dish!

Malaysian Char Kway Teow Beef Tacos

Ingredients:

For Char Kway Teow Beef:

- 1 lb beef steak (such as flank steak), thinly sliced
- 2 tablespoons vegetable oil
- 3 cloves garlic, minced
- 2 eggs, beaten
- 1 tablespoon soy sauce
- 1 tablespoon oyster sauce
- 1 tablespoon sweet soy sauce (kecap manis)
- 1 teaspoon chili paste or sambal oelek (adjust to taste)
- 1 teaspoon shrimp paste (optional)
- 1 teaspoon sugar
- Salt and pepper to taste
- 8 oz flat rice noodles (kway teow), soaked in warm water for 15 minutes and drained
- 1 cup bean sprouts
- 1 cup Chinese chives or green onions, cut into 2-inch lengths
- Lime wedges, for serving

For Tacos:

- 8 small soft taco shells or tortillas
- Sliced cucumber
- Sliced red chili (optional)
- Chopped cilantro
- Fried shallots (optional)
- Lime wedges, for serving

Instructions:

1. Prepare Char Kway Teow Beef:
    - Heat vegetable oil in a large skillet or wok over high heat.
    - Add minced garlic and stir-fry until fragrant.
    - Push garlic to the side of the skillet and add beaten eggs. Scramble until just set, then mix with the garlic.
    - Add thinly sliced beef to the skillet and stir-fry until browned.
    - In a small bowl, mix together soy sauce, oyster sauce, sweet soy sauce, chili paste, shrimp paste (if using), sugar, salt, and pepper. Pour over the beef mixture and stir well.
    - Add drained rice noodles to the skillet and toss until evenly coated with the sauce.

- Stir in bean sprouts and Chinese chives or green onions. Cook for another 1-2 minutes until the vegetables are tender and the noodles are heated through.
2. Assemble the Tacos:
    - Warm the taco shells or tortillas according to package instructions.
    - Spoon a generous amount of Char Kway Teow Beef onto each taco shell.
    - Top with sliced cucumber, sliced red chili (if using), chopped cilantro, and fried shallots (if using).
    - Serve with lime wedges on the side for squeezing over the tacos.
3. Serve:
    - Serve the Malaysian Char Kway Teow Beef Tacos immediately, while the beef is hot and the toppings are fresh.

These tacos offer a delicious fusion of flavors, combining the rich and savory Char Kway Teow with the freshness of taco toppings. Enjoy the bold Malaysian-inspired twist on this beloved Mexican dish!

Korean Galbi Short Rib Tacos

Ingredients:

For Galbi Short Ribs:

- 1 lb beef short ribs, cut into thin slices across the grain
- 1/2 cup soy sauce
- 1/4 cup brown sugar
- 2 tablespoons sesame oil
- 2 tablespoons rice vinegar
- 4 cloves garlic, minced
- 1 teaspoon ginger, grated
- 2 green onions, chopped
- 1 tablespoon sesame seeds
- 1/4 teaspoon black pepper
- 1 tablespoon vegetable oil, for cooking

For Tacos:

- 8 small soft taco shells or tortillas
- Shredded lettuce or cabbage
- Thinly sliced cucumber
- Sliced green onions
- Kimchi, for serving (optional)
- Sriracha mayo or Korean gochujang mayo, for serving (optional)

Instructions:

1. Marinate the Galbi Short Ribs:
    - In a bowl, combine soy sauce, brown sugar, sesame oil, rice vinegar, minced garlic, grated ginger, chopped green onions, sesame seeds, and black pepper.
    - Add the sliced beef short ribs to the marinade and toss until evenly coated. Cover and refrigerate for at least 1 hour, or overnight for best results.
2. Cook the Galbi Short Ribs:
    - Heat vegetable oil in a skillet or grill pan over medium-high heat.
    - Remove the marinated short ribs from the marinade, shaking off any excess.
    - Cook the short ribs in the skillet for 2-3 minutes on each side, or until browned and cooked through.
3. Assemble the Tacos:
    - Warm the taco shells or tortillas according to package instructions.
    - Place a few slices of cooked Galbi Short Ribs onto each taco shell.

- Top with shredded lettuce or cabbage, thinly sliced cucumber, and sliced green onions.
- Serve with kimchi on the side, if desired.
4. Optional: Serve with Sauce:
    - Drizzle Sriracha mayo or Korean gochujang mayo over the tacos for extra flavor and spice.
5. Serve:
    - Serve the Korean Galbi Short Rib Tacos immediately, while the beef is hot and the toppings are fresh.

These tacos offer a delightful fusion of savory and sweet flavors from the marinated short ribs, perfectly complemented by the fresh taco toppings. Enjoy the Korean-inspired twist on this beloved Mexican dish!

Thai Massaman Curry Beef Tacos

Ingredients:

For Massaman Curry Beef:

- 1 lb beef stew meat, cubed
- 2 tablespoons Massaman curry paste (store-bought or homemade)
- 1 can (14 oz) coconut milk
- 1 onion, sliced
- 2 potatoes, peeled and cubed
- 1 carrot, peeled and sliced
- 1 tablespoon fish sauce
- 1 tablespoon brown sugar
- 1 tablespoon tamarind paste
- 1/2 cup beef broth
- Salt and pepper to taste
- Chopped peanuts and fresh cilantro for garnish (optional)

For Tacos:

- 8 small soft taco shells or tortillas
- Sliced red onion
- Sliced cucumber
- Chopped cilantro
- Lime wedges, for serving

Instructions:

1. Prepare Massaman Curry Beef:
    - In a large skillet or pot, heat some oil over medium-high heat.
    - Add Massaman curry paste to the skillet and cook for about a minute until fragrant.
    - Add beef cubes to the skillet and brown them on all sides.
    - Stir in sliced onions and cook until softened.
    - Pour in coconut milk, beef broth, fish sauce, brown sugar, and tamarind paste. Stir well to combine.
    - Add cubed potatoes and sliced carrots to the skillet. Bring the mixture to a simmer.

- Cover and cook for about 1 hour, or until the beef is tender and the vegetables are cooked through. Stir occasionally and add more broth if needed.
- Season with salt and pepper to taste.
2. Assemble the Tacos:
    - Warm the taco shells or tortillas according to package instructions.
    - Place a spoonful of Massaman Curry Beef onto each taco shell.
    - Top with sliced red onion, sliced cucumber, and chopped cilantro.
3. Serve:
    - Serve the Thai Massaman Curry Beef Tacos immediately, with lime wedges on the side for squeezing over the tacos.
    - Garnish with chopped peanuts and fresh cilantro if desired.

These tacos offer a delightful blend of Thai curry flavors with the freshness of taco toppings. Enjoy the fusion of Thai and Mexican cuisines in every delicious bite!

Japanese Gyoza Tacos

Ingredients:

For Gyoza Filling:

- 1/2 lb ground pork
- 1 cup finely chopped cabbage
- 2 green onions, finely chopped
- 2 cloves garlic, minced
- 1 teaspoon grated ginger
- 1 tablespoon soy sauce
- 1 tablespoon sesame oil
- 1/2 teaspoon sugar
- Salt and pepper to taste

For Gyoza Tacos:

- Gyoza wrappers (or small flour tortillas as a substitute)
- Vegetable oil for frying
- Shredded lettuce or cabbage
- Sliced cucumber
- Sliced radishes
- Sliced green onions
- Sriracha mayo or soy sauce for drizzling
- Toasted sesame seeds for garnish
- Lime wedges for serving

Instructions:

1. Prepare Gyoza Filling:
    - In a bowl, combine ground pork, finely chopped cabbage, green onions, minced garlic, grated ginger, soy sauce, sesame oil, sugar, salt, and pepper. Mix well until thoroughly combined.
2. Assemble Gyoza Tacos:
    - Take a gyoza wrapper and spoon a small amount of the gyoza filling into the center.
    - Moisten the edges of the wrapper with water, then fold it over to create a half-moon shape. Pinch and pleat the edges to seal the gyoza.
    - Repeat with the remaining gyoza wrappers and filling.
3. Cook Gyoza Tacos:
    - Heat a skillet over medium heat and add a small amount of vegetable oil.
    - Place the gyoza in the skillet, flat side down, and cook for 2-3 minutes until the bottoms are golden brown.

- Carefully pour about 1/4 cup of water into the skillet and cover with a lid. Allow the gyoza to steam for 3-4 minutes, or until cooked through and the wrappers are translucent.
- Remove the lid and let any excess water evaporate. Cook for an additional 1-2 minutes until the bottoms are crispy again.

4. Assemble Tacos:
    - Place a cooked gyoza taco on a plate.
    - Top with shredded lettuce or cabbage, sliced cucumber, sliced radishes, and sliced green onions.
    - Drizzle with sriracha mayo or soy sauce.
    - Garnish with toasted sesame seeds.
5. Serve:
    - Serve the Japanese Gyoza Tacos immediately, with lime wedges on the side for squeezing over the tacos.

These tacos offer a delightful combination of crispy gyoza wrappers and flavorful pork filling, topped with fresh and crunchy vegetables. Enjoy the fusion of Japanese and Mexican cuisines in this unique dish!

Vietnamese Bun Cha Pork Tacos

Ingredients:

For Bun Cha Pork:

- 1 lb ground pork
- 3 cloves garlic, minced
- 2 shallots, finely chopped
- 2 tablespoons fish sauce
- 1 tablespoon soy sauce
- 1 tablespoon honey or brown sugar
- 1 tablespoon vegetable oil
- 1 teaspoon ground black pepper
- 1 teaspoon sesame oil
- 1/2 teaspoon crushed red pepper flakes (optional)

For Tacos:

- 8 small soft taco shells or tortillas
- Vermicelli noodles, cooked according to package instructions
- Shredded lettuce or cabbage
- Sliced cucumber
- Sliced carrots
- Fresh mint leaves
- Fresh cilantro leaves
- Lime wedges, for serving

For Dipping Sauce:

- 1/4 cup fish sauce
- 2 tablespoons rice vinegar
- 2 tablespoons water
- 2 tablespoons sugar
- 1 clove garlic, minced
- 1 Thai chili, thinly sliced (optional)

Instructions:

1. Prepare Bun Cha Pork:
    - In a bowl, combine ground pork, minced garlic, chopped shallots, fish sauce, soy sauce, honey or brown sugar, vegetable oil, ground black pepper, sesame oil, and crushed red pepper flakes (if using). Mix well to combine.

- Let the pork mixture marinate for at least 30 minutes, or refrigerate overnight for best results.
2. Cook Bun Cha Pork:
    - Heat a skillet or grill pan over medium-high heat.
    - Add the marinated pork mixture to the skillet and cook, breaking it apart with a spoon, until browned and cooked through, about 6-8 minutes.
    - Remove from heat and set aside.
3. Prepare Dipping Sauce:
    - In a small bowl, whisk together fish sauce, rice vinegar, water, sugar, minced garlic, and sliced Thai chili (if using) until the sugar is dissolved. Set aside.
4. Assemble Tacos:
    - Warm the taco shells or tortillas according to package instructions.
    - Place a spoonful of cooked Bun Cha Pork onto each taco shell.
    - Top with cooked vermicelli noodles, shredded lettuce or cabbage, sliced cucumber, sliced carrots, fresh mint leaves, and fresh cilantro leaves.
5. Serve:
    - Serve the Vietnamese Bun Cha Pork Tacos with lime wedges on the side for squeezing over the tacos.
    - Serve the dipping sauce on the side for dipping or drizzling over the tacos.

These tacos offer a delightful blend of savory and aromatic flavors, complemented by the freshness of the vegetables and herbs. Enjoy the fusion of Vietnamese Bun Cha with the handheld convenience of tacos!

Chinese Mapo Tofu Tacos

Ingredients:

For Mapo Tofu:

- 1 block (14 oz) firm tofu, cut into small cubes
- 2 tablespoons vegetable oil
- 2 cloves garlic, minced
- 1-inch piece of ginger, grated
- 2 green onions, chopped
- 2 tablespoons doubanjiang (spicy bean paste)
- 1 tablespoon chili bean paste (toban djan)
- 1 tablespoon soy sauce
- 1 teaspoon sugar
- 1 cup chicken or vegetable broth
- 1 tablespoon cornstarch mixed with 2 tablespoons water (slurry)
- Salt and pepper to taste
- Sichuan peppercorns, toasted and ground (optional)
- Chopped green onions and cilantro for garnish

For Tacos:

- 8 small soft taco shells or tortillas
- Shredded lettuce or cabbage
- Thinly sliced cucumber
- Sliced red bell pepper
- Sliced green onions
- Sriracha or chili garlic sauce for serving (optional)

Instructions:

1. Prepare Mapo Tofu:
    - Heat vegetable oil in a large skillet or wok over medium heat.
    - Add minced garlic, grated ginger, and chopped green onions to the skillet. Stir-fry for 1-2 minutes until fragrant.
    - Add doubanjiang and chili bean paste to the skillet. Stir-fry for another minute.
    - Stir in soy sauce and sugar.

- Add cubed tofu to the skillet and gently stir to coat with the sauce.
- Pour in chicken or vegetable broth. Bring to a simmer and cook for 5-7 minutes.
- Stir in the cornstarch slurry and cook until the sauce has thickened.
- Season with salt and pepper to taste. If desired, sprinkle with ground Sichuan peppercorns for extra flavor and numbing sensation.
- Remove from heat and set aside.

2. Assemble the Tacos:
   - Warm the taco shells or tortillas according to package instructions.
   - Place a spoonful of Mapo Tofu onto each taco shell.
   - Top with shredded lettuce or cabbage, thinly sliced cucumber, sliced red bell pepper, and sliced green onions.
3. Serve:
   - Serve the Chinese Mapo Tofu Tacos immediately, with sriracha or chili garlic sauce on the side for those who prefer extra spice.
   - Garnish with chopped green onions and cilantro.

These tacos offer a delightful fusion of spicy and savory flavors from the Mapo Tofu, perfectly complemented by the freshness of the taco toppings. Enjoy the unique blend of Chinese and Mexican cuisines in this delicious dish!

Indian Chana Masala Tacos

Ingredients:

For Chana Masala:

- 2 cups cooked chickpeas (or 2 cans, drained and rinsed)
- 2 tablespoons vegetable oil
- 1 onion, finely chopped
- 3 cloves garlic, minced
- 1-inch piece of ginger, grated
- 2 tomatoes, finely chopped
- 1 green chili, finely chopped (optional)
- 1 tablespoon ground coriander
- 1 teaspoon ground cumin
- 1 teaspoon turmeric powder
- 1/2 teaspoon garam masala
- 1/2 teaspoon paprika
- 1/4 teaspoon cayenne pepper (adjust to taste)
- Salt to taste
- Fresh cilantro leaves, chopped, for garnish
- Lemon wedges, for serving

For Tacos:

- 8 small soft taco shells or tortillas
- Shredded lettuce or cabbage
- Diced tomatoes
- Chopped red onion
- Chopped cilantro
- Greek yogurt or raita, for serving (optional)

Instructions:

1. Prepare Chana Masala:
   - Heat vegetable oil in a large skillet over medium heat.
   - Add chopped onion and cook until soft and translucent.
   - Stir in minced garlic, grated ginger, and chopped green chili (if using). Cook for another 1-2 minutes until fragrant.
   - Add chopped tomatoes to the skillet and cook until they break down and become pulpy.
   - Stir in ground coriander, ground cumin, turmeric powder, garam masala, paprika, and cayenne pepper. Cook for 1-2 minutes until the spices are fragrant.

- Add cooked chickpeas to the skillet and mix well with the spice mixture.
- Season with salt to taste and simmer for 5-10 minutes until the flavors meld together and the chickpeas are heated through.
- Garnish with chopped cilantro before serving.

2. Assemble the Tacos:
    - Warm the taco shells or tortillas according to package instructions.
    - Spoon a generous amount of Chana Masala onto each taco shell.
    - Top with shredded lettuce or cabbage, diced tomatoes, chopped red onion, and chopped cilantro.
3. Serve:
    - Serve the Indian Chana Masala Tacos with lemon wedges on the side for squeezing over the tacos.
    - Offer Greek yogurt or raita on the side for those who want to add a creamy element to their tacos.

These tacos offer a delightful blend of aromatic spices and hearty chickpeas, perfectly complemented by the freshness of the taco toppings. Enjoy the fusion of Indian and Mexican flavors in this delicious dish!

Malaysian Hainanese Chicken Rice Tacos

Ingredients:

For Hainanese Chicken:

- 1 whole chicken (about 3-4 lbs)
- 6 cups water
- 2 slices ginger
- 2 cloves garlic, smashed
- 2 stalks green onions, cut into halves
- Salt, to taste

For Rice:

- 1 cup jasmine rice, rinsed and drained
- 2 cups chicken broth (from cooking chicken)
- 1 slice ginger
- 1 clove garlic, minced
- Salt, to taste

For Sauce:

- 2 tablespoons soy sauce
- 1 tablespoon sesame oil
- 1 tablespoon oyster sauce
- 1 tablespoon ginger, grated
- 1 tablespoon garlic, minced
- 1 tablespoon green onion, finely chopped
- Salt and pepper, to taste

For Tacos:

- 8 small soft taco shells or tortillas
- Sliced cucumber
- Sliced tomatoes
- Chopped cilantro
- Sriracha or chili sauce, for serving (optional)

Instructions:

1. Cook Hainanese Chicken:
    - In a large pot, bring water to a boil. Add ginger, garlic, green onions, and salt.

- Carefully add the whole chicken to the pot, breast side down. Bring the water back to a boil, then reduce the heat to low, cover, and simmer for about 30-40 minutes, or until the chicken is cooked through.
- Once cooked, remove the chicken from the pot and plunge it into a bowl of ice water to stop the cooking process. Let it cool completely, then chop into serving pieces.

2. Prepare Rice:
   - In a saucepan, heat a little oil over medium heat. Add minced garlic and ginger slice, and sauté until fragrant.
   - Add the rinsed jasmine rice and stir for a minute until coated with the oil.
   - Pour in the chicken broth and bring to a boil. Reduce heat to low, cover, and simmer for about 15-20 minutes, or until the rice is cooked and the liquid is absorbed. Fluff with a fork and set aside.
3. Make Sauce:
   - In a small bowl, combine soy sauce, sesame oil, oyster sauce, grated ginger, minced garlic, chopped green onion, salt, and pepper. Mix well.
4. Assemble Tacos:
   - Warm the taco shells or tortillas according to package instructions.
   - Place a spoonful of cooked jasmine rice onto each taco shell.
   - Top with sliced Hainanese chicken pieces.
   - Add sliced cucumber and tomato on top.
   - Drizzle with the prepared sauce.
   - Garnish with chopped cilantro.
   - Serve with sriracha or chili sauce on the side for those who desire extra spice.
5. Serve:
   - Serve the Malaysian Hainanese Chicken Rice Tacos immediately, while the chicken and rice are still warm.

These tacos offer a delightful fusion of tender Hainanese chicken, fragrant rice, and flavorful sauce, all wrapped up in a convenient taco shell. Enjoy the unique blend of Malaysian and Mexican cuisines in this delicious dish!